SKYBOX PRESS • SAN DIEGO

Introduction
10

CHAPTER 1
1966–1970
12

CHAPTER 2
1971–1978
48

CHAPTER 3
1979–1988
88

CHAPTER 4
1990–1999
128

CHAPTER 5
2000–2007
172

CHAPTER 6
2008–Present
210

INTRODUCTION
Arthur Blank

Dear Friends,

June 30, 1965 will always be a date the city of Atlanta will hold dear. Rankin M. Smith was awarded a franchise on that day and pro football would become a fixture in this great city from that day forward. Officially, Atlanta became the 23rd professional football club in existence, the 15th in the NFL prior to the merger. You, the fans, chose the name that was given to the franchise. A school teacher from Griffin, Georgia, Julia Elliott, had the winning submission and said, "The falcon is proud and dignified, with great courage and fight. It never drops its prey. It's deadly and has a great sporting tradition." Truer words could not have been spoken, and they still ring true to this day.

One of the greatest moments in my life was December 6, 2001. On that day, I reached a preliminary agreement with the Falcons' Taylor Smith to purchase the team. As the current steward of the Falcons, I hope you enjoy a trip through the past 50 years in this book. It gives us all a chance to reflect on great moments and the players who are an indelible part of franchise history, such as: Steve Bartkowski, Tommy Nobis, Mike Kenn, Claude Humphries, Deion Sanders, Jessie Tuggle, Michael Turner, Roddy White, John Abraham, Matt Ryan and Julio Jones to name just a few.

We have continued to produce a team that you can be proud of not only on the field, but off the field as well. We have experienced unmatched success for this franchise since 2008, and our future expectations and aspirations are to bring championships to the city of Atlanta. I believe in our coaching staff and front office that we have to provide us the pieces we need to get that done. I have always said that my only goal is to bring a Lombardi Trophy to this city and my drive and determination to get that done is higher than ever.

This franchise has experienced a number of incredible moments during our 50 years, but I have no doubt our best moments are still ahead. I hope each of you enjoy this book as you reminisce over some of the memories that have forged our franchise and fan base.

Finally, I cannot thank you enough for your continued support of our team and I look forward to our continued journey together as we strive to bring a championship to Atlanta.

Rise Up!

Arthur M. Blank

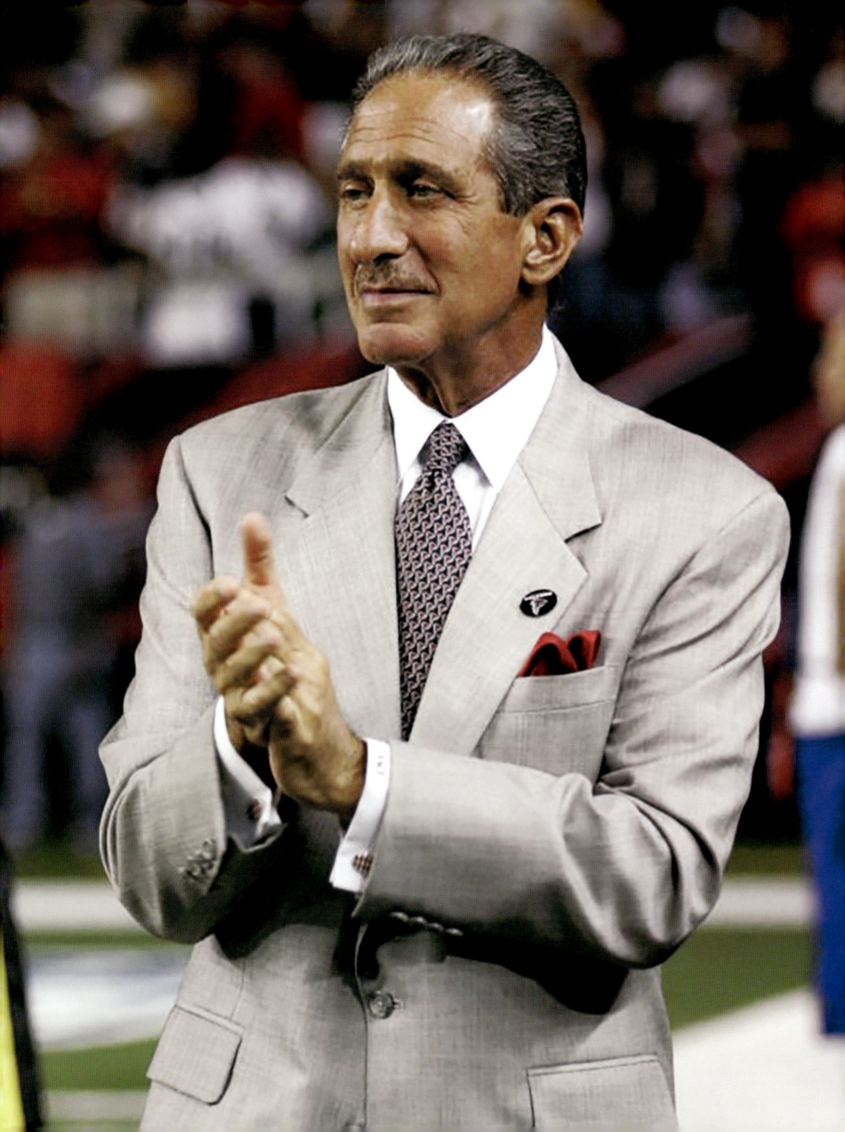

CHAPTER

1

1966–1970

As Atlanta weathered the growing pains of a booming metropolis emerging from the height of the civil rights movement, visions for a better future were kaleidoscopically influencing the city. The South needed a city to lead the way, and Atlanta undertook this steep challenge. Through leadership, philosophies, and unbreakable determination, a disciplined progress helped foster remarkable and widespread growth over the next 50 years.

In the midst of the transformation, bringing an NFL team to Atlanta had become an emphasis on the city's conversant wish list. Atlanta mayor Ivan Allen Jr. first promised to build a sports facility to attract a Major League Baseball team during his election campaign in 1961. After fruitless attempts to move a team, Allen was finally able to confirm that a club had verbally committed to make the move in 1964. A groundbreaking ceremony for what was originally named Atlanta Stadium began on April 15, 1964, and less than a year later (April 9, 1965), the Milwaukee Braves and the Detroit Tigers christened the $18 million stadium with an exhibition game.

The Braves officially arrived from Milwaukee for the 1966 season with a young Hank Aaron to lead the way, but more assemblages were needed for an NFL team to also make "the Launching Pad" its new home. Just months after the completion of Atlanta Stadium, however, Atlanta succeeded and was awarded an NFL franchise on June, 30, 1965.

The objective was evident: to serve the South's deep love for sports by bringing the NFL to Atlanta and establishing a football presence in the South that would promote the city's growth on a national scale. Unlike in the case of the arrival of the Braves, however, Atlanta's new NFL team had to build itself completely from the ground up.

Carl Sanders, governor of Georgia at the time, emphasized the importance of bringing the credibility of the NFL to Atlanta. Sanders made it his mission to pursue a team, and he succeeded with the help of Rankin Smith, an executive vice president at the Life Insurance Company of Georgia at the time, who paid a then-unprecedented $8.5 million to acquire Atlanta's NFL franchise. Smith immediately endeared himself to aficionados of the sport by asking a now-famous rhetorical question at the press conference following his acquisition of the franchise: "Doesn't every adult male in America want to own his own football team?"

Less than three months after Smith purchased the franchise, the team announced the winner of a contest to determine the name of the new team: Julia Elliott, a schoolteacher from Griffin,

OPPOSITE Rankin M. Smith, Sr., an insurance executive, paid $8.5 million to bring NFL football to his hometown of Atlanta.

Georgia, branded the new franchise the Falcons. Several other entrants suggested the name as well, but Elliott was declared the winner because of her reasons behind the name: "The falcon is proud and dignified, with great courage and fight. It never drops prey. It is deadly and has a great sporting tradition."

With the name now intact, Norb Hecker was pegged as the team's first coach. The inaugural season began with the 1966 NFL Draft, when the Falcons held the first pick in every round, along with an extra compensatory pick at the end of each of the first five rounds.

With the first pick in franchise history, the team selected Tommy Nobis, a two-time All-American linebacker at the University of Texas and winner of the Outland Trophy and the Maxwell Award. (Nobis, also drafted by the Houston Oilers of the American Football League, decided to ink his contract in Atlanta instead.) The merger of the NFL and AFL was not revealed until June 8, 1966. Under the merger agreement, the leagues played out separate regular-season schedules for the next four seasons (1966–1969) before officially merging into a two-conference solitary league in 1970.

The 1966 season kicked off as the Falcons hosted the Los Angeles Rams in the franchise's first game. The Rams took a 16-0 lead with a pair of Bruce Gossett field goals and a Jack Snow touchdown catch from Roman Gabriel before Atlanta answered right back with the franchise's first touchdown as Randy Johnson found Gary Barnes for a 53-yard score. Johnson ran in a touchdown that cut it to 16-14, but the Rams added a third-quarter field goal and held on 19-14, though Lee Calland intercepted Gabriel to record the franchise's first pick.

The inaugural season opened with nine losses, but a trip to take on the New York Giants in the 10th game of the season proved to be historic, providing the first spark of winning that has carried over into the 49 seasons since. Atlanta took a 13-3 lead into the half and opened the third quarter with Randy Johnson's third touchdown pass— the first multiple-touchdown passing game in Atlanta history—to take a 20-3 lead. The Falcons answered a Giants touchdown with a Johnson rushing score and held on for the 27-16 win. The victory opened a four-game stretch that saw the team record three wins.

The Falcons took their lumps in their opening season, as they scored only 204 points and allowed 437, but the promising finish and the 3-11 record were the start of an illustrious career for Nobis and the many all-time greats who would help shape this franchise. Nobis was elected to the Pro Bowl and was named Rookie of the Year after setting the unofficial record for most tackles in a season with a staggering 294, which still stands today. Even more impressive, Nobis accomplished that feat in just a fourteen-game season.

Atlanta's second season resulted in a 1-12-1 record and a last-place finish in the new Coastal Division of the NFL Western Conference with the Los Angeles Rams, the Baltimore Colts, and the San Francisco 49ers. The 1968 season also got off to a rough start, and after dropping its first three games, Atlanta turned to Norm Van Brocklin to take over as head coach for the final 11 games. The Falcons went 2-9 but made tremendous strides that were strengthening a tradition and setting up the organization for its first winning seasons. The Falcons drafted defensive end Claude Humphrey in the third overall pick of the 1968 draft, and in doing so, the team brought in a Hall of Fame talent who earned league-wide praise.

Nobis had established his role as the face of the franchise, and Humphrey was on his way to becoming one of the most feared pass rushers to ever play the game, but surrounding the star players with as much athleticism as possible was the franchise's focus for the first years. Atlanta's 1969 first-round draft pick, George Kunz, recalled the team's frantic search for more athletes when he ran into Randy Matson, 1968 Olympic gold medalist in the shot put, talking with the Falcons about a possible tryout during one of his visits to Atlanta before the 1969 draft.

Kunz gave the Falcons a 6-foot-5 tackle to anchor the line when he was taken off the board with the second pick of the 1969 draft and went on to make eight Pro Bowls during his 12-year NFL career. The Falcons improved to a 6-8 finish during his rookie season, which included a season sweep of the 49ers and the franchise's first win over the New Orleans Saints (45-17). That last victory marked one of the best individual performances of the first 50 seasons of

the Falcons. An NFL hat trick, in which a player passes, runs, and catches a touchdown in the same game, has been done only seven times in the history of the league. Atlanta's Harmon Wages notched his by throwing a 16-yard touchdown pass to Paul Flatley in the first quarter, running for a 66-yard touchdown for his first score, and then catching an 88-yard touchdown pass from Bob Berry in the second quarter.

The following season saw Atlanta lose another eight games, but a pair of ties kept the win total at just four games with a 4-8-2 finish. The 1970 season was also the birth of the NFC West, as the Saints joined the Falcons in that division for the first time. Atlanta opened the season with a 14-3 win in New Orleans in front of a crowd of more than 77,000 fans and completed its first season sweep over the rival Saints with a 32-14 Week 6 win in Atlanta.

In just five seasons, the Falcons were a competitive franchise, with some of the greatest individuals to play the game leading the exciting new journey. The efforts involved in building a franchise from the ground up are not driven by a pursuit of short-term results. An understanding that the foundation is the perpetuity of the original vision and the catalyst to support the future motivated the organization during these essential early years.

Van Brocklin once pointed to Nobis's locker and proclaimed, "There's where our football team dresses." This tale continues to get passed down through the franchise's history, as Nobis set the standard for each guy to put on the uniform behind him as the first Falcon. Nobis, along with Humphrey, was inducted into the Falcons Ring of Honor in the 2004 inaugural class. Both the University of Texas and the Falcons retired his number 60, making him the first and last Atlanta player to ever wear the now-legendary number. Overall, Nobis spent more than 40 years as a member of the organization, first on the field and later in the front office.

"If you are going to start a franchise, you are going to start with a defense," explained Kunz. "And if you are going to start with a defense, you are going to start with a signal caller, and Tommy was all of that. Tommy is the epitome of the type of person a franchise could build on, and I do not know if you can actually give anybody a bigger compliment than that."

ABOVE Tommy Nobis, the first ever draft pick of the expansion Falcons, checks out a picture of Atlanta Stadium with team owner Rankin Smith and Nobis's then girlfriend and future wife, Lynn Edwards.

ABOVE NFL Commissioner Pete Rozelle presents Rankin Smith with the Certificate of Membership for the league's 15th franchise.

OPPOSITE Rozelle notes Atlanta's having selected Tommy Nobis No. 1 overall in the 1965 draft. The Texas Longhorns star was also drafted by the AFL's Houston Oilers, but Nobis chose to play in the NFL and sign with the Falcons.

1ST ROUND

ATLANTA   TOM NOBIS (TE
LOS ANGELES
PITTSBURGH
PHILADELPH

ST. LOUIS
DETROIT
NEW YORK
AN FRANCISCO
HICAGO
REEN BAY
LEVELAND
BALTIMOR

GREATEST MOMENTS

1

WELCOME TO ATLANTA
6/30/1965

Rankin Smith, an executive vice president at the Life Insurance Company of Georgia at the time, paid a then-unprecedented 8.5 million dollars to bring an NFL team to Atlanta. With the motives of bringing more growth to the city, Smith brought the prestige of the National Football League to the Southeast's key metropolis. Smith immediately endeared himself to aficionados of the sport by asking a now-famous rhetorical question at the press conference following his acquisition of the franchise: "Doesn't every adult male in America want to own his own football team?" Touché, Mr. Smith.

Dignitaries mark the christening of the first game in franchise history on September 11, 1966 versus the Los Angeles Rams.

A real falcon (above) and the Falconettes (below) were all part of the festivities.

GREATEST MOMENTS

2

TEACHER OF THE YEAR
9/29/1965

Less than three months after Rankin Smith purchased the franchise, the team finished a contest used to determine the name of the new franchise. Julia Elliott, a schoolteacher from Griffin, Georgia, won the naming game, branding the new franchise the Falcons. Several other entries suggested the name, but Elliott was declared the winner of the contest because of her reasons behind the name: "The Falcon is proud and dignified, with great courage and fight. It never drops prey. It is deadly and has a great sporting tradition."

GREATEST MOMENTS

3

INTRODUCING MR. FALCON
11/27/1965

The Falcons used the first overall pick of the draft and the franchise's first selection to pick up Tommy Nobis. The Texas linebacker won **NFL Rookie of the Year** honors after amassing an inconceivable and franchise-record 294 combined tackles. In 11 professional seasons, he led the Falcons in tackles nine times and went to five Pro Bowls, including one in 1972 after two knee surgeries. He was named **All-Pro** twice, made the **NFL's All Decade Team** for the 1960s, and became the first player enshrined into the Falcons Ring of Honor.

Tommy Nobis lived up to the hype and won Rookie of the Year honors in 1966.

GREATEST MOMENTS

4

A NEW ERA KICKS OFF
9/11/1966

The Falcons hosted the Los Angeles Rams at Atlanta Stadium in the franchise's first game. The Rams took a 16-0 lead with a pair of Bruce Gossett field goals and a Jack Snow touchdown catch from Roman Gabriel. Atlanta answered right back with the franchise's first touchdown as Randy Johnson found Gary Barnes for a 53-yard score. Johnson ran in a touchdown that cut it to 16-14, but the Rams added a third-quarter field goal and held on 19-14. Lee Calland intercepted Gabriel to record the franchise's first pick.

The first touchdown in Falcons history was a 53-yard pass from quarterback Randy Johnson, above, to receiver Gary Barnes. Atlanta battled back from a 16-0 deficit, but the Rams went on to win 19-14.

ABOVE Head coach Norb Hecker takes the field with (left to right) Randy Johnson, Jimmy Sidle, and Vern Burke.

OPPOSITE Teammates Alex Hawkins and Perry Lee Dunn.

Halfback Junior Coffee fights for yards against Baltimore Colts defenders in the 1967 season opener.

Greg Brezina (50) and Mike Freeman (43) tackle star back Lem Barney in a 1968 game versus the Detroit Lions.

RING OF HONOR

TOMMY NOBIS

PLAYED
1966–1976

INDUCTED
2004

In 1966, the Atlanta Falcons used the first pick in franchise history to select two-time All-American linebacker Tommy Nobis, winner of the Outland Trophy and the Maxwell Award in 1966, from the University of Texas. Nobis, who was also the top pick in the AFL draft before choosing the Falcons, was elected to the Pro Bowl his rookie season after being named Rookie of the Year and set the unofficial record for most tackles in a season with an untouchable 294. He produced five Pro Bowl appearances during his 11-season career and is represented on the NFL's 1960s All-Decade Team.

Nobis was inducted into the Falcons Ring of Honor in the 2004 inaugural class. Both the University of Texas and the Falcons retired his number, making "Mr. Falcon" the only Atlanta player to wear the now-legendary number 60. Nobis, who founded the Tommy Nobis Center in 1975, which provides job training and employment services for youth and adults with disabilities, won the Joseph P. Kennedy Jr. Award for his activism and his work with the Georgia Special Olympics, and he was named the NFL Man of the Year. He is retired after spending over 40 years as a member of the Falcons organization.

"Tommy is the epitome of the type of person a franchise could build on," franchise great George Kunz, drafted in 1969 by the Falcons and a teammate of Nobis for six seasons, said. "I do not know if you can actually give anybody a bigger compliment than that."

Jerry Simmons (above and left), played parts of three seasons for the Falcons in the late 1960s.

OPPOSITE Tommy Nobis accepts the Texas Sports Writers Association's Professional Athlete of the Year award in 1968.

ABOVE One of the original Falcons, cornerback Ken Reaves played eight seasons with Atlanta and had 29 interceptions.

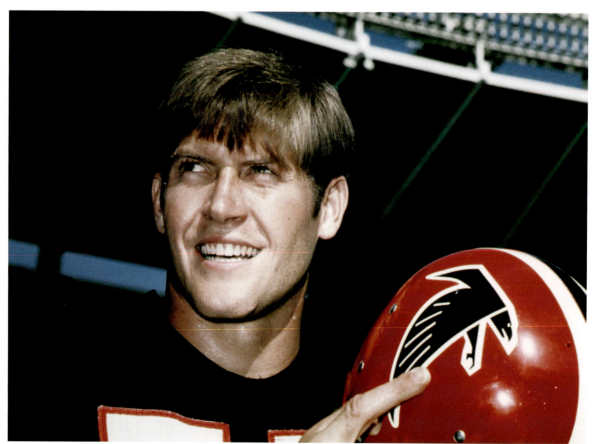

TOP Tight end Jim Mitchell played 11 seasons from 1969-1979 for the Falcons earning Pro Bowl honors in 1969 and 1972.

BOTTOM With the No. 2 overall pick in 1969, Atlanta drafted Notre Dame's George Kunz, who would go on to make eight Pro Bowls during his 11 seasons in the NFL.

GREATEST MOMENTS

5

A TASTE OF VICTORY
11/30/1966

The Falcons' first season opened with nine losses, but a trip to take on the Giants in the 10th game of the season proved to be historic and sparked confidence that has carried over into the 49 seasons since. Atlanta took a 13-3 lead into the half and opened the third quarter with Randy Johnson's third touchdown to take a 20-3 lead. The Falcons answered a Giants touchdown with a Johnson rushing score and held on for a 27-16 win. The victory opened a four-game stretch that saw the team record three wins.

GREATEST MOMENTS

6

WAGES DOES IT ALL
12/7/1969

Only seven NFL players have managed a hat trick—passing, running, and catching a touchdown in the same game—in the league's history. Atlanta's Harmon Wages notched his against the New Orleans Saints in 1969 as the Falcons torched their rivals 45-17. Wages threw a 16-yard touchdown pass to Paul Flatley in the first quarter, then caught an 88-yard touchdown pass from Bob Berry in the second quarter to build a 21-3 lead. His 66-yard touchdown run increased the lead to 45-10.

Undrafted running back Harmon Wages scored 10 touchdowns in his five-year NFL career, all with the Falcons.

ABOVE In 1968, Tommy Nobis and the Atlanta defense welcomed future Hall of Famer Claude Humphrey, the No. 3 overall pick out of Tennessee State.

OPPOSITE Linebacker Greg Brezina spent 11 seasons with the Falcons; in 1969 he led the league in fumble recoveries and was named to the Pro Bowl.

CHAPTER 2

1971–1978

Survival is the rudimentary prerequisite of success, and after surviving five NFL seasons, the Falcons franchise was equipped for its first taste of success. From 1971 to 1978, Atlanta reached for new milestone after new milestone and effectively hallmarked the era with the team's earliest major accomplishments.

The Falcons secured their first winning season (7-6-1) in 1971 with a 24-20 victory over New Orleans in the final week of the regular season, a feat that escaped the rival Saints until their 21st year in the League with a strike-shortened 1987 season. The season included winning their first nationally televised game, a Monday Night Football contest in late November, as the Falcons beat the Packers 28-21 at Atlanta–Fulton County Stadium—the first time the whole country had a chance to look at the franchise.

Atlanta's winning season did not result in a playoff berth, but the positive momentum carried over into the 1972 season and helped the franchise match the win total with a 7-7 finish. The 1972 season also conceived a storyline and personal milestone that lasted for another four years. The Falcons had yet to see a running back join the 1,000-yard club, and during the final week in a game against the Kansas City Chiefs, it looked like Dave Hampton would be the first back to eclipse 1,000 yards. With 1,001 yards already gained, he was tackled for a 6-yard loss on his last carry of the game and finished the year at 995 yards. He came up just short in 1973 with 997 yards before finally hitting 1,002 yards in 1975, after missing the 1974 season with injuries, and was named NFL Comeback Player of the Year.

The Falcons opened the 1973 season in New Orleans and left with a 62-7 victory, the most lopsided final score in the history of the Falcons-Saints rivalry. Atlanta finished the year with a new franchise-best 9-5 record but once again sat on the other side of the playoff fence. From 1971 to 1973, however, the Falcons showed the league that they were no longer just surviving and could compete with the NFL's elite.

When the Falcons spoiled the Carolina Panthers' perfect regular season in 2015 with a 20-13 Week 16 victory, it was the first time since the 1973 season that the Falcons had defeated the NFL's last unbeaten team. The 1972 Miami Dolphins had finished the NFL's only perfect season, and the 9-0 Minnesota Vikings had sights set on their own gridiron immortality the following year when they visited the Falcons. Atlanta took a 20-7 lead into the fourth quarter, but Minnesota cut the lead to 20-14 and marched toward a potential game-winning touchdown. Hall of Fame quarterback Fran Tarkenton, however, was forced out of bounds on the deciding fourth-down play as the Falcons held on.

OPPOSITE Quarterback Steve Bartkowski from the University of California was drafted No. 1 overall in 1975 and ushered the Falcons into a new era.

The run of three straight seasons without a losing record was forcefully snapped in 1974, as Hampton's injury was one of many that decimated Atlanta's offense. The Falcons scored only 111 points during the 1974 season and reached the end zone just a dozen times, the lowest total in franchise history and the second lowest by any team in a fourteen-game NFL season. An anemic offense and painful losses, like a 42-7 midseason beating dished out by the Dolphins, led to Van Brocklin's dismissal after the season and prompted a much-needed changing of the guard under center.

These changes would be made through the 1975 draft as Atlanta used a defining trade to bring in a franchise quarterback. Atlanta's first-round pick in 1969 (No. 2 overall), George Kunz, would be the key to creating the trade. Kunz and sixth-round pick Fulton Kuykendall were moved to Baltimore in exchange for the No. 1 overall pick, which Atlanta used to welcome Cal quarterback Steve Bartkowski to Atlanta.

Bartkowski was brought in to fix the offensive woes, but the search for a head coach continued until Marion Campbell was hired. Campbell went 4-10 his first season and after a 1-4 start in 1976, he was replaced by Pat Peppler, who went 3-6 en route to Atlanta's second straight 4-10 record. After recording 23 wins from 1971 to 1973, Atlanta won just 11 games over the next three seasons.

Humphrey's injuries in 1975 also contributed to the team's struggles, and the severity of his knee injury led many to believe the setback was potentially career ending. After returning to post a career-best 15 sacks in 1976, however, Humphrey proved he was back to spearheading the Falcons defense.

"People projected that [1975] was the end of my football career," said Humphrey, "that I wouldn't play anymore—that I couldn't. I had torn both cartilages in my knee, and it was over for me. My football career was down the drain."

After a porous defense in 1976 that surrendered 59 points in one occasion, first-time head coach Leeman Bennett was hired, and with assistant Jerry Glanville, he created a scheme that would change the franchise—and ultimately transform league rules. The defensive style would earn the name "the Gritz Blitz," a system that included a play called "Sticky Sam" that would send nine players rushing the quarterback. Atlanta was able to put together the greatest single-season defensive performance in NFL history, giving up only 129 points, a record that still stands today.

"They were fun to watch," said Bartkowski "They were flying around—it was exciting to

ABOVE Leeman Bennett was the mastermind behind the record-setting "Gritz Blitz" defense in 1977.

be on that football team with the kind of guys we had playing. There weren't any stars, just a collective group with a lot of interchangeable pieces, just getting it done week in and week out."

As good as the defense was, the offense continued to struggle. The Falcons scored more than 17 points only twice during the 1977 season and finished the year 7-7 despite having what is regarded as the stingiest defense of the Super Bowl era.

Before the 1978 season, the Falcons moved into a state-of-the-art facility in the suburb of Suwanee and added one of the most important players in franchise history as Atlanta selected offensive tackle Mike Kenn with the 13th pick. Kenn, who started all 16 games for the Falcons as a rookie left tackle and was named to the NFL all-rookie team, ended up playing his entire 17-year career with the Falcons (1978–1994) and set the franchise record for games started and games played with 251.

After several seasons of inconsistencies on one or both sides of the football, the offense made big enough plays on the defensively dominant 1978 team to produce one of the most exciting seasons in franchise history. Donning sleek new uniforms, the Falcons scored 240 points that season—15 points per game, the lowest total in franchise history for a 16-game season. Despite those struggles, Atlanta continued to find ways to win.

In the heart of a five-game winning streak that turned a 2-4 start around, an unlikely hero took center stage as the Falcons scored a 15-7 win in Week 9 over the division-leading Los Angeles Rams on Monday Night Football. Kicker Tim Mazzetti was bartending at a Smokey Joe's near the University of Pennsylvania six games into the 1978 season before the Falcons signed him. His heroic season included making 13 of 16 FGs and a team-record 11 in a row, as well as kicking 4 game-winning field goals. In the Monday-night win over the Rams, Mazzetti went 5-for-5 to lead the 15-7 victory.

Atlanta defeated the 49ers 21-10 the following week to move to 6-4. This only raised the stakes for two matchups in the next three weeks against the Saints, who were also in the hunt for their first playoff berth. The Falcons won both contests 20-17, but the first meeting, on November 12 in New Orleans, produced what remains one of the franchise's all-time greatest moments.

A historic comeback began with 2 minutes and 23 seconds left as the Falcons trailed 17-6. Bartkowski engineered an 80-yard drive that was capped off by a 1-yard touchdown run by Haskel Stanback that brought the game to 17-13. The defense got the offense the ball back, but the four-game winning streak was in serious jeopardy. Time was running out, and the Falcons were on their own 43-yard line when they called "Big Ben Right" in the huddle to set up a desperation heave down the right sideline. However, this was not a conventional Hail Mary. As planned, Bartkowski launched the ball deep where receiver Wallace Francis was there to tip it in the air. The perfectly tipped ball was corralled by a trailing Alfred Jackson, who sprinted in the final 10 yards for the game-winning 57-yard score with just 19 seconds left.

"Big Ben Right is where I just throw it up and hope," said Bartkowski. "I was surprised. I was able to see the whole play, and my first reaction was, 'Praise the Lord.'"

A 9-7 season put the Falcons in the playoffs for the first time in franchise history, and Atlanta hosted Philadelphia in the first NFC wild card game. Once again, the team used Bartkowski's late-game magic, this time to erase a 13-0 fourth-quarter deficit. Eagles quarterback Ron Jaworski threw a 13-yard touchdown pass to Harold Carmichael for the Eagles' first touchdown, but Philadelphia missed the extra point. Running back Wilbert Montgomery's touchdown run gave the Eagles a 13-0 lead heading into the fourth quarter. Atlanta had just five minutes left when Bartkowski found Jim Mitchell for a 20-yard touchdown pass to make it 13-7. Unlike "Big Ben Right," where Francis was the assist man to Jenkins, the speedy receiver was targeted in crunch time for this game winner. Francis hauled in the deciding score on a 37-yard touchdown pass from Bartkowski to complete the comeback and stamp the first playoff win in team history.

The Falcons led the Dallas Cowboys 20-13 at halftime of the divisional playoff the following week but were outscored 14-0 in the second half, and the postseason run ended with a 27-20 loss.

There was a lot to take away from the 1978 season, but with an assemblage of franchise greats leading the core of the roster and playoff success now on the club's résumé, the Falcons confidently approached a new chapter.

GREATEST MOMENTS

7

THE FIRST WINNING SEASON
12/19/1971

Atlanta entered the final game of the regular season 6-6-1 and would have to win at New Orleans and complete the season sweep to capture the franchise's first winning season at 7-6-1. Saints starting quarterback Archie Manning ran in a score to take a 17-10 lead, but Atlanta knotted it up with an Art Malone touchdown run to open the fourth. The Saints reclaimed a 20-17 lead with a 36-yard field goal, but Falcons quarterback Bob Berry found Ken Burrow for a 22-yard game-winning touchdown to stamp the 24-20 victory and winning year.

Dick Shiner holds for placekicker Bill Bell, who made 60 of 62 extra point attempts in his two years with Atlanta.

OPPOSITE Warren Bryant was a stalwart on the Falcons offensive line during eight seasons wearing the red and black.

ABOVE Defensive end Claude Humphrey made life miserable for offensive opponents who crossed his path.

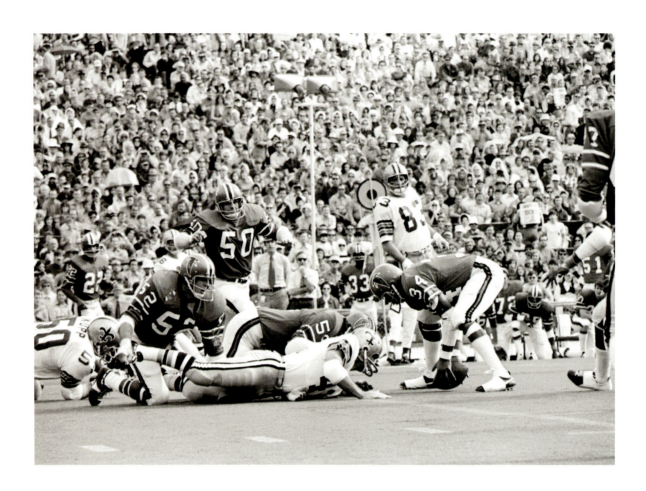

TOP Falcons safety Ray Brown picks up a fumble by Saints running back Jim Strong during a 1971 game versus New Orleans.

BOTTOM Brown upends Saints quarterback Archie Manning in that same game, which the Falcons won 24-20.

GREATEST MOMENTS

8

SEASON-OPENING SAINTS SMACKDOWN
9/16/1973

The Falcons visited New Orleans to open the 1973 season and left with a 62-7 victory, the most lopsided loss in the history of the Falcons-Saints rivalry. Dick Shiner tossed a pair of touchdowns to Ken Burrow and a third passing touchdown to Wes Chesson. Eddie Ray got in on the action with a touchdown pass and a touchdown run in the fourth quarter. Nick Mike-Mayer kicked two field goals, and Art Malone and Joe Profit rushed for touchdowns. Atlanta's defensive touchdown came on a Tom Hayes 65-yard interception return. Atlanta finished the year 9-5, the franchise's best record until 1980.

OPPOSITE Defensive ends Claude Humphrey and John Zook both made the Pro Bowl in 1973.

ABOVE Rolland "Bay" Lawrence hauls in one of his franchise-record 39 career interceptions.

RING OF HONOR

CLAUDE HUMPHREY

PLAYED
1968–1978

INDUCTED
2008

Claude Humphrey spent the first 10 years of his 13-year pro football career with the Atlanta Falcons, and after 28 years of eligibility, he finally entered the Pro Football Hall of Fame in August 2014. Humphrey, the No. 3 pick of the 1968 NFL Draft, established his place in the pros early, earning Defensive Rookie of the Year.

Humphrey spearheaded the infamous Falcons "Grits Blitz" defense in 1977, which was designed to terrorize quarterbacks. The result was a defense that gave up the fewest points in NFL history (129 in 14 games, 9.2 PPG). The following year, the league changed its rules to better serve the offense, and Humphrey and the Falcons' success were key factors.

Humphrey transformed the game and helped pave the way for some of the NFL's top pass rushers, like Reggie White, Bruce Smith, and fellow 2014 inductee Michael Strahan. He ended his career with the Eagles (1979–1981) and retired with 126.5 career sacks in 171 career games played and had five All-Pro seasons.

What was most impressive about the pass rusher, however, was the injury he overcame in 1975 after being sidelined for the entire season. Many thought the setback could be career ending, but Humphrey returned to post a career-best 15 sacks in 1976 before leading Atlanta's record-setting defense in 1977.

"People projected that [1975] was the end of my football career—that I wouldn't play anymore, that I couldn't," said Humphrey. "I had torn both cartilages in my knee, and it was over for me. My football career was down the drain."

Guard Dick Enderle, above, and tight end Mike Donohoe, below, played for the Falcons in the late 1960s and early 1970.

GREATEST MOMENTS

9

SPOILING PERFECTION
11/19/1973

Miami had finished the NFL's only perfect season in 1972, and the 9-0 Vikings had their sights set on perfection the following year as they visited the Falcons for a *Monday Night Football* showdown. Atlanta took a 20-7 lead into the fourth quarter, but Minnesota eventually cut the margin to 20-14 and was looking to keep the perfect season alive with a touchdown. Hall of Fame quarterback Fran Tarkenton, however, was forced out of bounds on the deciding fourth-down play. This remains one of the top 10 games when it comes to MNF ratings and the sole time the Falcons have defeated the NFL's last unbeaten team in a season.

Defensive end Jeff Merrow played 108 games at defensive end for Atlanta from 1975 to 1983.

Center Jeff Van Note spent 18 seasons with the Falcons, and his 225 games started ranks second in team history.

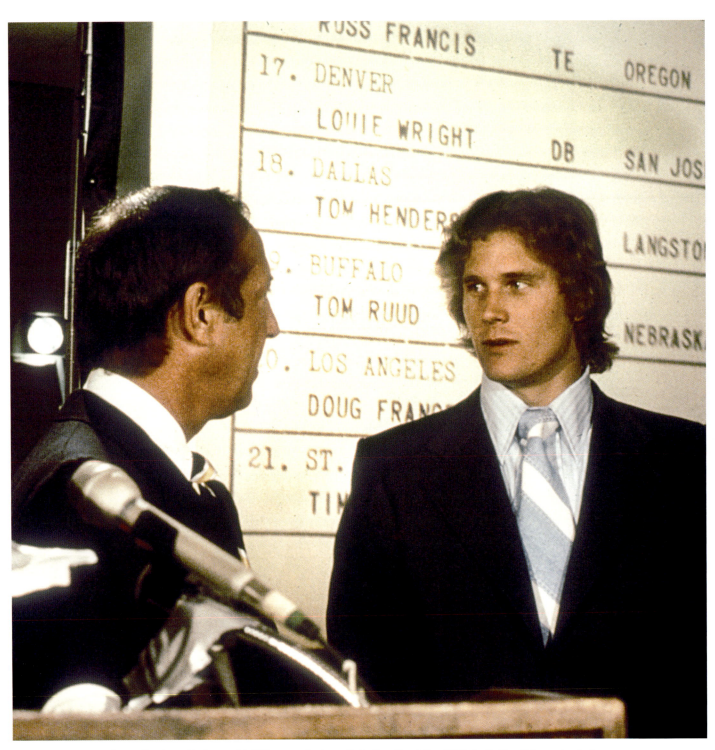
Steve Bartkowski chats with NFL commissioner Pete Rozelle at the 1975 draft. The Falcons traded up to select the quarterback from Cal, who played 11 seasons behind center in Atlanta.

GREATEST MOMENTS

10

FRANCHISE-DEFINING TRADE
1/28/1975

The Falcons desperately needed a franchise quarterback, but the 1975 draft was undeniably thin at that position. Baltimore held the first pick; the Colts had a franchise signal caller in Bert Jones, then just 23, but they extracted a steep price from Atlanta: perennial Pro Bowl offensive lineman George Kunz plus the No. 3 pick (which the Colts used to pick guard Ken Huff). In return, the Falcons selected Cal quarterback Steve Bartkowski No. 1 and also received a sixth-round pick, used to select UCLA linebacker Fulton Kuykendall, both of whom enjoyed decade-long, productive careers in Atlanta.

GREATEST MOMENTS

THE GRITZ BLITZ
1977 Season

After a porous defense in 1976 that surrendered 59 points on one occasion, first-time head coach Leeman Bennett was hired to lead the team, and with assistant Jerry Glanville, he created a scheme that would change the league forever. The defensive style, which earned the name "the Gritz Blitz," included a play called "Sticky Sam" that sent nine players rushing the quarterback. Atlanta put together the greatest single-season defensive performance in NFL history, giving up only 129 points, a record that still stands today.

Marion Campbell did two tours as the Falcons Head Coach, from 1974 to 1976 and 1987 to 1989.

ABOVE The Falcons of the 1970s finished as high as second in the division four times; in 1980, Atlanta would finally win its first division title.

OPPOSITE "Mr. Falcon," Tommy Nobis.

GREATEST MOMENTS

MAZZETTI'S MAGIC
10/30/1978

Tim Mazzetti was bartending at Smokey Joe's near the University of Pennsylvania six games into the 1978 season until the Falcons signed him. His season included making 13 of 16 FGs and a team-record 11 in a row, as well as kicking four game-winning FGs. In the memorable Monday-night game against the division-leading Rams, Mazzetti went 5-for-5 to give the Falcons a 15-7 victory. As a result, the Falcons made it to the playoffs for the first time, as a wild card, that year. During the game, Howard Cosell exclaimed, "This Philadelphia bartender won't need to mix scotch-and-waters any longer."

TOP Norm Van Brocklin took over as Head Coach three games into the 1968 season and led the Falcons for seven years.

BOTTOM Despite battling injuries throughout his career, Steve Bartkowski started 121 of the 123 games in which he appeared over 11 seasons with the Falcons.

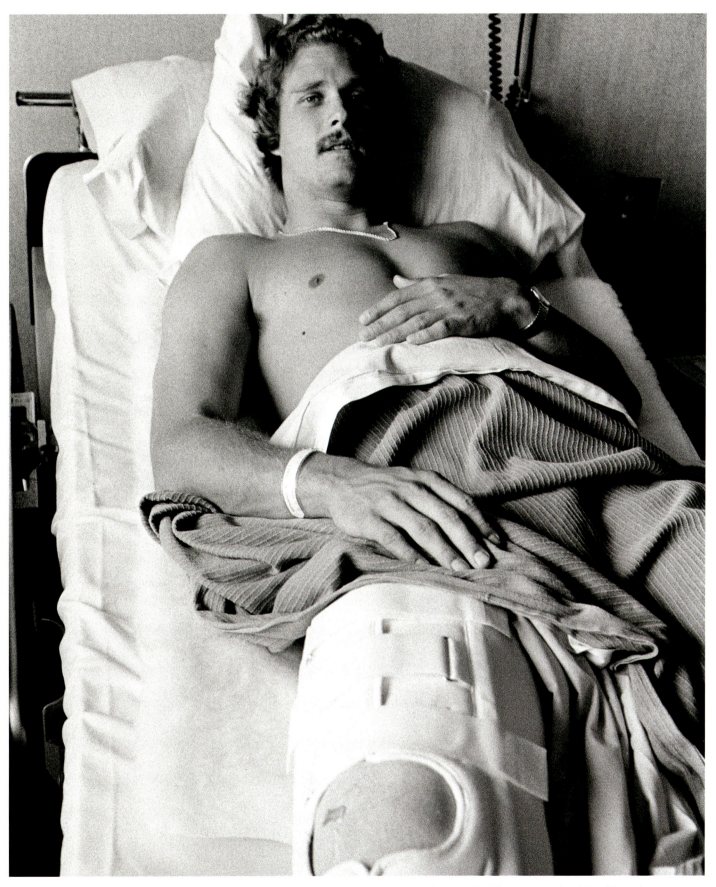

OPPOSITE Rookie defensive lineman Wilson Faumuina shows no mercy to future Hall of Fame quarterback Joe Namath during his swan song with the Rams.

ABOVE Steve Bartkowski played all 16 games only twice in his career, thanks in part to five operations on his right knee.

RING OF HONOR

STEVE BARTKOWSKI

PLAYED
1975–1985

INDUCTED
2004

The Falcons traded up and selected quarterback Steve Bartkowski with the No. 1 overall pick of the 1975 draft. He was headed to a Falcons organization that had posted only two winning seasons in its nine years, but his late-game heroics and leadership introduced the franchise to its first taste of playoff success.

In 1978, he led the organization to its first playoff appearance and win as the Falcons rallied for a 14-13 victory over the Eagles. In 1980, he threw for 3,544 yards and a career-high 31 touchdowns as the Falcons secured their first division title and added another divisional-playoff victory.

A highlight of Bartkowski's 12-year pro career is the play that forever will follow him: "Big Ben Right." It has been the most celebrated play in Falcons history for decades, and when the timing, significance, and excitement are all taken into account, it is easy to understand why. The Falcons were on their own 43-yard line when they desperately called "Big Ben Right" in the huddle. As planned, Bartkowski launched the ball deep down the right sideline, where receiver Wallace Francis was there to tip it in the air. The perfectly tipped ball was corralled by a trailing Alfred Jackson, who sprinted the final 10 yards for the game-winning 57-yard score.

"'Big Ben Right' is where I just throw it up and hope," said Bartkowski. "I was surprised. I was able to see the whole play, and my first reaction was, 'Praise the Lord.'"

Bartkowski, a 2004 Ring of Honor inductee, was on the Falcons Board of Directors until the 2015 season.

Saints quarterback Archie Manning, seen in action (top) and nursing a sore jaw (above), during a 1977 game at Fulton County Stadium, lost 16 of the 22 meetings between his Saints and the Falcons during his 11 seasons in New Orleans.

GREATEST MOMENTS

BIG BEN RIGHT
11/12/1978

The Falcons took a four-game winning streak into their Nov. 12 trip to New Orleans but faced a four-point deficit with time running out. In what will always be remembered as "Big Ben Right," Steve Bartkowski's heave to Wallace Francis was tipped into the hands of Alfred Jackson for a game-winning 57-yard touchdown with just 19 seconds left. The Falcons won 20-17 and the fans stormed the field and tore down the goalposts. Atlanta beat New Orleans at home by the same score two weeks later and reached the playoffs for the first time in franchise history with a 9-7 record.

OPPOSITE Running back Mike Esposito gains a first down before being tackled by Ed "Too Tall" Jones during a 1976 game in which the Falcons upset the Cowboys 17-10.

ABOVE Steve Bartkowski throws a pass over the Eagles' Dennis Harrison in the 1978 Wild Card game, the Falcons' first ever playoff game.

Atlanta fans tear down the goalposts after the Falcons' 14-13 come from behind to win in the 1978 Wild Card game versus Philadelphia.

GREATEST MOMENTS

14

FIRST PLAYOFF WIN
12/24/1978

The Falcons made the playoffs for the first time and hosted Philadelphia in the NFC Wild Card game. Eagles QB Ron Jaworski threw a 13-yard touchdown pass to Harold Carmichael for the Philadelphia's first touchdown, but they missed the PAT. Wilbert Montgomery's 1-yard touchdown run after halftime gave the Eagles a 13-0 lead heading into the fourth quarter. With five minutes left, quarterback Steve Bartkowski hit tight end Jim Mitchell for a 20-yard touchdown, and then found wide receiver Wallace Francis for a 37-yard score to complete the comeback, seal the victory, and stamp the first playoff win in Falcons history.

CHAPTER

3

1979–1988

During the 1980s, Atlanta football fans were graced with some of the greatest Falcons to ever suit up in the red, white, and black. Steve Bartkowski, William Andrews, Gerald Riggs, and Alfred Jenkins combined to give the Falcons one of the most explosive offenses the franchise has ever seen. Bartkowski set franchise records in passing that stood until Matt Ryan shattered them in 2013, and Riggs posted rushing records that are still intact to this day. In the trenches, young talents and veterans alike blossomed into perennial Pro Bowlers, with Jeff Van Note, Mike Kenn, Bill Fralic, and R. C. Thielemann all taking the field.

On defense, it was unforgettable players such as Rolland Lawrence, Don Smith, Buddy Curry, and Bobby Butler, and the beginning of the Jessie Tuggle and Deion Sanders era, who patrolled the gridiron. Special coaches, players, and teams littered the decade, but only twice did the Falcons finish with a winning record and a playoff appearance.

Following a promising 1978 playoff year, the Falcons started the 1979 season 2-0 with a thrilling 40-34 season-opening overtime win against the Saints at the Louisiana Superdome and a 14-10 Monday Night Football victory over the Eagles at Veterans Stadium. Atlanta looked like it was finally going to establish itself as an annual postseason contender.

The Falcons had an opportunity to move to 3-0 against the Denver Broncos when Bartkowski threw for a then-career-high total of 326 yards and two touchdowns, but Jim Turner buried a 24-yard field goal in overtime to lift Denver to a 20-17 victory. The loss spiraled Atlanta into a 2-9 tailspin that led to a 6-10 finish and a lost season.

The 1980 season didn't start as well, as the Falcons lost two of their first three games, but they found momentum after a 20-17 win at Candlestick Park against the San Francisco 49ers, a game that almost slipped away. Atlanta held a commanding 20-3 lead midway through the fourth quarter before Steve DeBerg caught fire. He hit Freddie Solomon for a 93-yard bomb and Earl Cooper for a 27-yard strike but ran out of time as the Falcons clung on. Bartkowski threw just 17 passes for 90 yards, unfathomable totals in today's game, as Head Coach Leeman Bennett elected to run the ball 38 times to chew up the clock and keep DeBerg off the field.

That seemingly unsuspecting win ignited an 11-1 stretch in which the Falcons ripped off nine straight wins. Atlanta rolled to a franchise-best 12-4 record and, more importantly, the team's first division championship, winning the NFC

OPPOSITE William Andrews burst into the NFL, earning four straight Pro Bowl appearances from 1980 to 1983.

West by one game over the 11-5 Los Angeles Rams. Bartkowski earned his first Pro Bowl selection after throwing for career numbers of 3,544 yards and 31 touchdowns, while Andrews enjoyed his best year to date with 1,308 rushing yards and garnered his first Pro Bowl nod as well. Atlanta boasted the fifth-best-scoring offense in the league at 25.3 points per game and had the third best in terms of total yards. Everything was clicking for the Falcons, with six players sent to the Pro Bowl, all from the offensive side of the ball.

January 4, 1981, was the date set for the divisional round featuring the host Falcons and the 12-4 Dallas Cowboys, who beat the Rams in the wild card game, 34-13. The date is forever etched in the brains of the Falcons faithful, and the three-plus hours were some of the most grueling Atlanta sports has ever witnessed.

Entering the fourth quarter, the Falcons looked to be in control, up 24-10 at Atlanta–Fulton County Stadium. Bartkowski had hit Alfred Jenkins for a 60-yard touchdown pass to take a 10-0 lead in the first quarter and found William Andrews from 12 yards away to take a 14-point lead into the final quarter.

Then the unthinkable happened.

"We sat on the ball and let them back in the game," explained Mike Kenn.

Robert Newhouse scored on a 1-yard plunge early in the fourth quarter to cut the lead to 24-17, but Tim Mazzetti tacked on a 34-yarder with 6:37 remaining to push the lead to 27-17. When Dallas' Danny White got the ball back under center, Atlanta's defense had no answer for the red-hot gunslinger, who finished 25 of 39 for 322 yards, three touchdowns, and one interception. White drove the Cowboys 62 yards, all through the air, and connected with Drew Pearson for a 14-yard score to make it 27-24.

"We went into a prevent defense, and Danny White just stood back there and could throw the ball to anyone," said Kenn.

White did just that, getting the ball back on the Cowboys' own 30 with 1:48 left to play after the Falcons were unable to move the ball on offense. White quickly moved the Cowboys into field goal range, but instead of playing it safe and working for the tie, he found Pearson once again, this time from 23 yards out, to take the lead.

Atlanta had one last opportunity, but Bartkowski was sacked for a 9-yard loss, and the Falcons eventually turned the ball over on downs. There were plenty of chances throughout the game for the Falcons to lengthen their lead, but it was one play that Kenn points to that changed the momentum.

"The big play came when it was third-and-one and we could have knocked two more minutes off the clock with a first down and we still had a two-touchdown lead," remembered Kenn. "We

ABOVE Tiger Greene (33) and Mike Pitts (74) sandwich Saints running back Earl Campbell during a 31-24 victory in 1985.

had a play called 'Zero 1 Trap,' which William Andrews ran and worked all year. But before the ball was snapped, Ed 'Too Tall' Jones stepped into the neutral zone, which was OK back then if you got back, but he never got back on his side before it was snapped. And he was right in the hole to make the play. I watched that film, and he was offsides."

Coach Bennett said after the loss, "It was a bitter pill to swallow. I still feel we're good enough to go to the Super Bowl. Any team that wins 12 games is good enough. But it's a very empty feeling losing in the playoffs."

The 1981 season saw the Falcons improve even more upon their offense, finishing second in the league in points per game at 26.6, but the team stumbled to a 7-9 year, missing the playoffs.

Atlanta's quest to become a perennial power was stunted yet again in 1982, this time due to a 57-day-long players' strike, which caused the regular season to be cut to just nine games.

The strike took place because the NFL Players Association (NFLPA) was not pleased with how revenue was being distributed. Owners, not willing to budge, felt like they deserved the bigger cut of the loot. In the end, a five-year agreement was put in place, with salary increases, bigger bonuses, and severance packages all awarded to the players.

Because of the shortened season, the NFL adopted a special 16-team playoff tournament after the settlement. Eight teams from each conference were seeded 1–8 based on their regular-season records; Atlanta cracked the playoffs with a 5-4 mark as the No. 5 seed.

On the field, Atlanta met Minnesota in the first round of the reconstructed playoffs. Up 24-23 in the fourth quarter, the Falcons once again had their hearts broken, losing 30-24 after a Ted Brown 5-yard run sealed a victory for the Vikings in the first playoff game played in the newly opened Metrodome.

The Falcons not only lost the game and ended their season, but they also lost Bennett, who, despite being the most successful coach in franchise history at the time, was fired after six seasons. Bennett, who had helped instill stability in the burgeoning franchise and felt blindsided by the move, told United Press International, "I have a feeling of being used. I have a feeling of betrayal. I thought we were in this thing together, but I was the guy let go."

With Bennett out, the team turned to Dan Henning to lead the way. Atlanta went 22-41-1 under Henning before rehiring Marion Campbell as head coach for the 1987 season. Campbell picked quite the year to return to the sidelines after last coaching Atlanta in 1976 and spending 1983–85 in Philadelphia.

The five-year agreement from the 1982 strike had run its course, and after Week 2 of the 1987 season, the players walked out again, this time for 24 days. The games scheduled for the third week of the season were canceled, reducing the 16-game season by a single game. Weeks 4–6 saw replacement players take the field, while just 15 percent of the NFLPA's players chose to play during the strike.

The product on the field greatly suffered, and attendance dropped severely and games became hard to watch. In the end, the owners ended up winning the standoff, but in the long run, it was an integral piece that helped get the ball rolling to begin free agency in the NFL.

Through all the turmoil of the 1987 season, Atlanta finished 3-12. The silver lining found through all of this was the signing of an undrafted 5-foot-11 free agent linebacker out of Valdosta State named Jessie Tuggle. "The Hammer" saw sparing time as a rookie, but something bigger was in store. Atlanta was beginning to plant seeds. Quarterback Chris Miller was selected that year along with future four-time Pro Bowl defensive back Elbert Shelley. The Falcons missed with the No. 1 pick in the 1988 draft, selecting Aundray Bruce, but the 1989 draft yielded them a game changer named Deion Sanders that put the franchise on the map and slowly began to build the Falcons into a legitimate franchise.

As a rookie, Sanders was also starting his professional baseball career, but he turned heads quickly on the football field as he returned his first punt with the Falcons for a touchdown to spark his Pro Football Hall of Fame career. The Falcons finished 3-13 in 1989, and Campbell retired after the 12th game, but good times were around the corner.

OPPOSITE Alfred Jenkins is congratulated after one of the 40 touchdowns he scored in a career spent entirely as a Falcon.

TOP William Andrews loses the handoff against the Colts.

Third-round draft pick William Andrews out of Auburn became a four-time All Pro before his career was cut short by a knee injury.

GREATEST MOMENTS

15

WELCOMING PARTY
9/2/1979

In his first career NFL game after being drafted in the third round by the Falcons, running back William Andrews broke the franchise record for rushing yards in a single game, covering 167 yards to help the Falcons capture a 40-34 overtime win against New Orleans in the Superdome. That season, Andrews rushed for 1,023 yards and started his career with three straight seasons of over 1,000 yards rushing. Only twice in his six-year career did he not crack that plateau, and one of his most memorable runs came in 1982 on a 86-yard catch-and-run in a 34-27 win over Denver when he took a screen pass and absolutely obliterated defensive back Steve Wilson along the way.

GREATEST MOMENTS

16

RAISE THE BANNER
12/14/1980

The Falcons' 15th season was filled with historic moments, including a 35-10 Week 15 victory over San Francisco that gave the franchise its first division title. The victory moved Atlanta to 12-4 and stood as the franchise record for most wins in a season until the 14-2 Super Bowl season in 1998. Quarterback Steve Bartkowski opened the game with a rushing touchdown and threw three more touchdowns before Al Richardson's fumble recovery built a commanding 35-3 lead. Earl Jones and Jeff Yeates each intercepted Joe Montana.

Cornerback Bobby Butler lays out Vikings wide receiver Sammy White during the first round of the playoffs in 1983.

Linebacker Buddy Curry (above) played his entire career in Atlanta, from 1980 to 1987, as did defensive end Mike Gann (opposite), from 1985 to 1993.

RING OF HONOR

JEFF VAN NOTE

PLAYED
1969–1986

INDUCTED
2006

From 1969 to 1986, one face never changed in Atlanta. It might have gotten a little older and a little more worn, but Jeff Van Note was the foundation and face of the franchise through thick and thin from when he was drafted in 1969 in the 11th round until he retired at the age of 40.

Originally drafted as a linebacker out of Kentucky, Van Note was quickly moved by Head Coach Norm Van Brocklin to center, where he would flourish for the next 18 seasons and garner six Pro Bowl selections, both franchise records. His 155 consecutive games played was also a record.

Van Note missed only four games during his career and snapped to an astounding 14 quarterbacks during his 18 years, in which he made three trips to the playoffs. Prior to his final game, the Falcons honored his number and presented him with a 1957 Chevy in front of fans at the Atlanta–Fulton County Stadium. Van Note was later inducted into the Georgia Sports Hall of Fame in 1999. After spending some time as a color commentator, Van Note was inducted into the Falcons Ring of Honor in 2006 and had his No. 57 jersey retired.

Van Note explained to the late Ralph Wiley of Sports Illustrated why he played so long in the physically demanding NFL: "I asked myself a long time ago why I wanted to play this game so bad so long. Money? I only made $12,000 when I started. Publicity? I played on one good team. Respect? No. I play because I love it. I needed something to love. Football was it."

All-Pro running back and kick returner James "Cannonball" Butler takes a handoff from Randy Johnson versus San Francisco.

TOP The No. 2 overall pick in the 1985 draft, Bill Fralic became a starter at offensive guard as a rookie and went on to make four Pro Bowls and twice earn First Team All-Pro honors.

BOTTOM A Falcon for 11 years, defensive back Scott Case led the league with 10 interceptions in his Pro Bowl year of 1988.

GREATEST MOMENTS

17

FOURTH QUARTER EXPLOSION
9/13/1981

The Falcons were coming off a franchise-best 12-win season and opened 1981 in fashion with a 27-0 victory over the Saints. Week 2, however, put the Falcons in a hole as the host Green Bay Packers took a commanding 17-0 lead into the fourth quarter. Atlanta stormed back and erased the deficit and then some with an NFL-record-tying 31 points in the fourth quarter. A Mick Luckhurst field goal, a William Andrews rushing touchdown, a Steve Bartkowski touchdown pass, and two defensive touchdowns left the Packers stunned as Atlanta ran away with a 31-17 victory.

GREATEST MOMENTS

18

BIG BEN II
11/20/1983

The Falcons stunned the Bill Walsh–led San Francisco 49ers 28-24 on a last-second 47-yard touchdown pass from Steve Bartkowski to Billy "White Shoes" Johnson. In a play dubbed "Big Ben Part II," Bartkowski launched a deep ball into a crowd, and it was deflected into Johnson's hands and brought in for the score. Bartkowski outplayed Joe Montana, throwing for 301 yards and two touchdowns. "White Shoes" caught six balls for 104 yards and the memorable score. The win avenged a 24-20 loss at the hands of the Niners earlier in the season.

William Andrews and Joe Montana shake hands after the Falcons beat the 49ers 17-7 in San Francisco in 1982.

Billy Johnson, from tiny Widener University in Chester, Pennsylvania, made three Pro Bowls and played 14 seasons in the NFL despite being a 15th round draft pick.

GREATEST MOMENTS

19

'WHITE SHOES' SHINES
9/8/1985

Atlanta–Fulton County Stadium was the scene for Billy "White Shoes" Johnson as he glided into the record books by becoming the NFL's all-time leader in punt-return yardage after gaining 58 yards in the season opener against the Detroit Lions. The electrifying and charismatic Johnson made three Pro Bowls and one All-Pro team over his 14-year career. During his illustrious return career, "White Shoes" brought back six punts and two kicks to the house. He also added a career-high 830 yards receiving and five scores in the 1985 season.

ABOVE Alfred Jenkins posted back-to-back Pro Bowl selections in 1980 and 1981 thanks to his ability to catch the ball and turn up field.

OPPOSITE Michael Haynes celebrates one of his 34 career receiving touchdowns with the Falcons.

OPPOSITE Mike Kenn was big, at 6'7", and durable, spending his entire 17-year career in Atlanta and starting all 251 games he played.

ABOVE Kenn and Steve Bartkowski at an informal Falcons practice at Norcross High School in September 1982.

Gerald Riggs breaks free during a 34-17 win at San Francisco in 1988, a game in which he rushed for 115 yards and a touchdown.

GREATEST MOMENTS

20

RIGGS RUNS WILD
12/22/1985

In the final game of the season, running back Gerald Riggs carried the ball 39 times for 158 yards to help the Falcons capture a 16-10 victory over the Saints in the Superdome. That performance marked his ninth 100-yard rushing game of the season as he finished the campaign with 1,719 yards, good for tops in the NFC. Riggs made the Pro Bowl that season, one of three appearances in his career. Twenty-seven years after he left Atlanta, Riggs' record for the all-time leading rusher remains intact, with 6,631 yards coming from 1,587 carries.

RING OF HONOR

WILLIAM ANDREWS

PLAYED
1979–1983, 1986

INDUCTED
2004

In 1979, the Atlanta Falcons selected William Andrews in the third round with the 79th overall pick. The complete back was a two-time state champion at Thomasville High School before heading to Auburn University when the Tigers were known as "Running Back U," producing the likes of Joe Cribbs and James Brooks.

Andrews played six healthy seasons with the Falcons, missing both the 1984 and 1985 seasons due to a severe knee injury in the preseason. When on the field, the 6-foot, 206-pound back was one of the league's best, collecting four straight Pro Bowl selections from 1980 to 1983. Andrews broke 19 team records and was just the second running back in NFL history to have two 2,000-yard (combined-yards) seasons—the first was O. J. Simpson. In his first five seasons, Andrews had more total yards (8,382) than any other player in the league.

He was admitted into the Falcons Ring of Honor in 2004, the team retired his No. 31, and he was inducted into the Georgia Sports Hall of Fame in 1996. Andrews ranks third all-time in Falcons rushing yards with 5,986.

Andrews' knee injury is what ultimately cut the powerful runner's career short: "It was tough, because there was a lot of nerve damage in the knee, and it takes a long time for the nerve to grow back," explained Andrews. "I had a great doctor in Dr. Andrews, and it was big just getting back on the field. But after 1986, the Falcons said I could stay and take a diminished role, and I didn't want that. I saw the handwriting on the wall, so I retired."

GREATEST MOMENTS

21

VAN NOTE RETIRES
12/21/1986

The 18 years that center Jeff Van Note played with the Falcons is a team record. He also leads the franchise in most consecutive games played with 155. Selected 262nd in the 11th round of the 1969 NFL Draft, Van Note made five Pro Bowls, and his tenure spanned so many years that he played with six of the other eight Ring of Honor inductees, as well as all three of the other Falcons whose numbers, like Van Note's No. 57, are retired. Fittingly, the final game of Van Note's storied career was a victory.

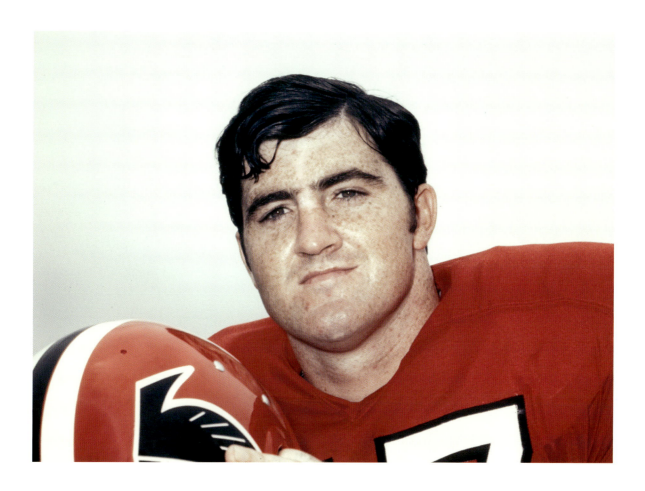

Jeff Van Note played 18 years in Atlanta, beginning at the age of 23 in 1969 and retiring at the age of 40 following the 1986 season.

ABOVE Falcons safety Tom Pridemore spent eight seasons in Atlanta, racking up 21 interceptions and 13 fumble recoveries.

OPPOSITE Linebacker Jim Laughlin celebrates a Falcons touchdown after defensive end Doug Rogers recovered a blocked punt in the end zone during the Wild Card playoff game at Minnesota on January 9, 1983.

OPPOSITE The Falcons selected Aundray Bruce out of Auburn with the No. 1 pick in the 1998 NFL draft.

ABOVE Bruce collected 16 sacks in his four seasons with the Falcons, including this take down of Joe Montana during Bruce's rookie season.

CHAPTER 4

1990–1999

The 1990s have been called the decade that transformed Atlanta. Chronologically, the start of an era or decade can always be compared to its end in order to gauge the extent of growth and change, but this hardly completes the story. There is the human element of change. For decades, the chatter and excitement that projected Atlanta's growth into a cultural and economic world city resonated and became a common goal and vision.

Before this became the decade that transformed Atlanta, it was just another era of opportunities. It took the city's well-established history of conceptualizing opportunities with supported plans of action to reach the growing global scale the city sees today.

During this era, Atlanta was able to transform from being considered a long-shot bid city in 1987 to the host of the 1996 Summer Olympic Games. The Falcons evolved from a franchise that had shared Atlanta–Fulton County Stadium for 26 years to the first "domed" team to reach a Super Bowl.

The structures, attitudes, and relics brought to existence from 1990 to 1998 represent an era defined by some of the city's most remarkable accomplishments. And like those traces from our modern past, the 1998 NFC Championship banner swaying proudly from the rafters today represents much more than a flash of time.

When the 1990 Falcons season kicked off, there was already a sense of a new beginning. It was the franchise's 25th season, and gone were the red helmets and white or red jerseys and in was a brand-new look, with black helmets, silver pants, and black or white jerseys. Also, Jerry Glanville returned to the city as head coach. He had served as the Falcons secondary coach in 1977–78 before climbing his way up the coaching ladder with the Houston Oilers and leading them to a playoff berth in 1989. A seven-game losing streak during the 1990 season, however, ended Atlanta's shot at the postseason, and Glanville and the Falcons finished with a 5-11 record.

Coming off a subpar season did not slow down a 1991 roster filled with All-Pros, future Hall of Famers, and emerging stars. Throughout the season, the Falcons were cheered on the sidelines by rapper M. C. Hammer, whose song "Too Legit to Quit" was adopted as their anthem. The determined Falcons doubled the win total from the previous season at 10-6, the franchise's best mark since it went 12-4 in 1980. Quarterback Chris Miller, right tackle Chris Hinton, receiver Andre Rison, and Hall of Famer Deion Sanders each made the Pro Bowl, while Jessie Tuggle finished with an NFL-best 207 tackles and Mike Kenn led the offensive line with an All-Pro effort. Deep threat Michael Haynes had a career season as well, leading the league with a reception average of 22.4 yards.

The 1991 season also brought the franchise its first on-the-road playoff win, and it came in New Orleans against the NFC West champs in

OPPOSITE Head Coach Jerry Glanville brought a renewed excitement to Atlanta when he took over the Falcons in 1990.

memorable fashion. Miller found Haynes for a game-winning 61-yard catch-and-run touchdown to beat the Saints 27-20. Miller threw for 291 yards and three touchdowns, while Haynes totaled six catches for 144 yards and two scores. Both Tim McKyer and Sanders recorded interceptions from future Falcon backup quarterback Bobby Hebert. This was the first of two monumental road-playoff wins this era would produce, but the latter would not come for another seven seasons.

Atlanta added a draft class that included Bob Whitfield and Chuck Smith before the 1992 season, but a 1-5 record in the NFC West kept the Falcons out of the playoffs with a 6-10 finish. Atlanta defeated the New York Jets 20-17 in their Georgia Dome debut on September 6, but the defensive struggles that buried the season became apparent soon after. The 1992 Falcons allowed the most points in the league (414) and placed last in total yards allowed (5,549), yards per play (5.9), rushing yards allowed (2,294), and yards per rushing attempt (4.9).

The 1993 season unwrapped an 0-5 start, but the team won five of its next six games to keep a potential turnaround in sight. The Falcons were unable to reach .500, however, and dropped to 5-7 with a 33-17 loss to Glanville's old team in Houston before sliding to a second straight 6-10 record. Glanville was fired following the season.

Atlanta acquired running back Jamal Anderson in the seventh round of the 1994 NFL Draft and brought in new head coach June Jones. Jones operated a run-and-shoot offense that was imbalanced his first season, as Anderson remained an unknown backup through his first two years. Atlanta took a league-low 330 carries in 1994 and, after a promising 4-2 start, lost 7 of the final 10 games and missed the playoffs for the 13th time in 14 seasons.

The 1995 season saw a return to the playoffs, as it all came down to the final week of the regular season. The Falcons held off the San Francisco 49ers 28-27 to earn a wild card berth at 9-7, but then Atlanta went one and done and fell to the Green Bay Packers 37-20 in a New Year's Eve loss at Lambeau Field.

An 0-8 start to the forgettable 1996 season led to a 3-13 season and Jones' dismissal. The silver lining of the season came with Anderson, who established his place as a reliable feature back. Anderson improved from 161 rushing yards in 1995 to a 1,055-yard effort in 1996, the first of his three back-to-back seasons in which he eclipsed 1,000 yards.

On January 21, 1997, Dan Reeves was hired as new head coach. The team got off to an 0-5 start his first year, but a 7-4 record the rest of the way built confidence and a sense of direction the organization needed to embark on the most successful season of its first 50 years the following fall.

There were several particularly significant moments during the 1998 NFC Championship season, but the incredible run seemingly took on a life of its own during a Week 10 trip to New England, which ended Atlanta's string of 22 straight losses at cold-weather stadiums. (It was during this game that the infamous Dirty Bird dance was created. The dance soon swept the NFL, as everyone from players to fans to even coaches began to show off their Falcon-inspired moves.) Anderson ran for 104 yards and two touchdowns to power the Falcons to a 41-10 drubbing of the Patriots. It was another noteworthy performance for Anderson, who would account for 1,846 rushing yards while scoring 16 total touchdowns during the 1998 season.

Coming off the win over the Pats was another test for the surging Dirty Birds. Including a rematch of a 31-20 Week 3 loss earlier in the season at San Francisco, the Falcons had lost five straight contests to its division rival. In front of 70,000-plus fans at the Georgia Dome for their Week 11 matchup, however, the Falcons reversed the curse and beat Steve Young, Jerry Rice, and crew 31-19. The Atlanta defense, led by Tuggle, held the 49ers to just 76 yards on the ground. Tuggle scooped up a fumble and returned it for a touchdown early in the fourth quarter to put Atlanta up 24-6.

The Falcons won their last nine games of the regular season and entered the playoffs as the No. 2 seed with a franchise-best 14-2 record. But if that wasn't dramatic enough, there was another element to this story. After Week 14, Coach Reeves was diagnosed with multiple blockages to his coronary arteries, a condition that would require quadruple bypass surgery.

Reeves disregarded the warning signs in hopes of finishing the season but fortunately still got checked out just in time. Doctors stated that by the time he checked in, he was within hours of

what could have been a catastrophic heart attack. As defensive coordinator, Rich Brooks took over as head coach during Week 15 and 16, but Coach Reeves returned for the regular-season finale and was back to lead the team into the playoffs.

After a bye in the first round, Atlanta beat the 49ers again in the divisional round 20-18, but an even taller task was waiting in the NFC Championship game at the Hubert H. Humphrey Metrodome with a 16-1 Vikings team. In what remains the greatest win in Falcons history and one of the most shocking upsets in NFL playoff history, the Falcons prevailed despite falling behind 20-7 in the second quarter. Minnesota later held a 27-20 lead and had a chance to ice the game in the closing minutes of regulation, but Vikings kicker Gary Anderson missed his first field goal of the season on a 38-yard attempt. The Falcons took advantage of a rare miscue by one of the best teams of the modern era and quarterback Chris Chandler found Terrance Mathis in the end zone with 49 seconds left to send it to overtime.

The Falcons defense came up with a stop to start the extra period and the Vikings were forced to punt the ball back into the hands of Chandler and the fervent Falcons offense. Chandler drove down the field and set up a 38-yard Morten Andersen field goal that went through the uprights and clinched the 30-27 victory.

The Falcons were now headed to Super Bowl XXXIII in Miami, and like the Braves had done earlier in the decade, the team energized the city. Just like before the game against the Vikings, not many gave the Falcons much of a chance against the Denver Broncos and John Elway, and what weighed even heavier on the team was that star safety Eugene Robinson was arrested for soliciting a prostitute the night before the game.

The Falcons tried to put the Robinson matter aside and briefly led the Broncos 3-0 in Super Bowl XXXIII after an Andersen field goal, but a Howard Griffith touchdown run and an 80-yard touchdown pass from Elway to Rod Smith grew a 17-6 halftime deficit. The teams went scoreless in the third quarter before Denver added touchdown runs by Griffith and Elway to make it 31-6. Atlanta responded with a Tim Dwight 94-yard kickoff-return touchdown and a Chandler touchdown pass to Mathis but fell short 34-19.

Denver took the Super Bowl title, but the Falcons run to football's biggest stage produced an extensive transformation for the franchise to carry into the new millennium.

ABOVE The creator of the "Dirty Bird" dance, Jamal Anderson celebrates the Falcons 30-27 overtime victory in the NFC Championship over the Vikings in January 1999.

Deion Sanders began his Hall of Fame career as the fifth overall pick of the Falcons in the 1989 draft.

GREATEST MOMENTS

PRIMETIME PERFORMANCE
9/10/1989

Rookie Deion Sanders returned his first punt in the 1989 season opener against the Los Angeles Rams 68 yards for a touchdown. Five days earlier, "Prime Time" had hit two doubles, smashed a homerun, scored twice, and had four RBIs playing left field for the New York Yankees. A man of many talents and nicknames, "Neon Deion" is regarded as one of the best two-sport athletes of all time.

OPPOSITE Two-sport star Deion Sanders played 14 seasons in the NFL and parts of nine seasons in Major League Baseball, including 1991 to 1994 with the Atlanta Braves.

ABOVE Jerry Glanville worked closely with the Falcons defense as Head Coach after coaching that side of the ball for Atlanta from 1977 to 1982.

ABOVE Jessie Tuggle stuffs future Hall of Famer Barry Sanders, who managed just 44 yards on 12 carries when Atlanta beat Detroit 34-22 in November 1995.

OPPOSITE Andre "Bad Moon" Rison hauls in a Jeff George pass for a touchdown—one of 56 TDs Rison scored in five seasons as a Falcon.

GREATEST MOMENTS

ROAD WARRIORS
12/28/1991

The Falcons notched their first road victory in the playoffs as quarterback Chris Miller hit wide receiver Michael Haynes for a game-winning 61-yard catch-and-run score to beat the rival New Orleans Saints in the Wild Card Round 27-20. Miller threw for 291 yards and three touchdowns in the win, while Haynes totaled six catches for 144 yards and two scores. Both Tim McKyer and Deion Sanders recorded interceptions off future Falcons backup quarterback Bobby Hebert. Atlanta finished the year at 10-6, the franchise's best mark since it went 12-4 in 1980.

Chris Miller from the University of Oregon was a first round draft pick in 1987 and played seven seasons with the Falcons.

RING OF HONOR

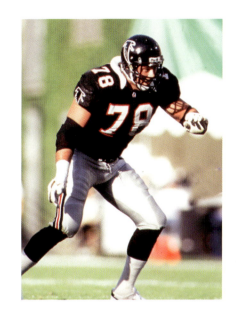

MIKE KENN

PLAYED
1978–1994

INDUCTED
2008

Mike Kenn, who wore No. 78 and played all 17 years with the Falcons after being drafted 13th overall in the 1978 NFL Draft out of Michigan, was once praised by a future Hall of Fame head coach: "I've never seen any offensive tackle with his agility and quickness." Those words came from the late, great 49ers coach, Bill Walsh.

Kenn started in all 251 games he played for the Falcons, once playing in 94 consecutive games, and went to five straight Pro Bowls from 1980 to 1984. The athletic lineman quickly became a premier blocker, as he was selected to the All-Rookie team in 1978.

Kenn, inducted into the Falcons Ring of Honor in 2008, is the Falcons record holder for most games played and games started, providing the longevity and stability the growing franchise needed.

"It was great for me and my family but also for the people back home, because I came from a blue-collar area, and a lot of them were living vicariously through me being a football player," said Kenn of being honored by Atlanta.

At Kenn's Michigan Pro Day, Bill Curry, then coach of the Green Bay Packers, told Kenn that he wanted to draft him and convert him into a tight end. If he had slipped to the Packers, Kenn says, his career would have been much different: "The irony of it all is that if I would have been taken by the Packers and moved to tight end, I don't think I would have ever lasted 17 years in the NFL."

"The Hammer" Jessie Tuggle quickly became a fan favorite after transforming himself from an undrafted rookie into a hard-hitting All-Pro linebacker.

GREATEST MOMENTS

24

IT'S HAMMER TIME
1991 Season

Undrafted out of Valdosta State in 1987, linebacker Jessie "The Hammer" Tuggle proved the scouts all wrong. He was not tall by NFL standards, at 5' 11", but he was fierce and durable, playing 14 seasons, leading the league in tackles (207) in 1991, and becoming the Falcons' all-time leader in total tackles with 2,065. A five-time Pro Bowler and member of the team's Ring of Honor inaugural Class of 2004, Tuggle's tenacity and toughness made his a fan favorite and Falcons legend.

Head coach June Jones and quarterback Jeff George talk strategy during their shared debut with the Falcons in the 1994 regular season opener at Detroit, which Atlanta lost in overtime 31-28.

GREATEST MOMENTS

25

DOME SWEET DOME
9/6/1992

The Falcons won the season opener and Georgia Dome opener 20-17 over the visiting New York Jets in front of 65,585 fans who packed into the new stadium to see Atlanta kick off a new era of football in its new home. Though they were outgained by 105 yards, the Falcons controlled the clock. Quarterback Chris Miller led the charge, going 21-of-29 with 196 yards and two scores. Earlier in the year, during the preseason, Atlanta had welcomed the Philadelphia Eagles with a lineup of top musicians to kick off the Dome's first Falcons game: M. C. Hammer, John Denver, and Travis Tritt all performed throughout the night.

When the Georgia Dome opened in 1992, it was the world's largest covered stadium by capacity in the world.

OPPOSITE In his 14-year NFL career, all as a Falcon, Jessie Tuggle amassed 1,640 tackles.

ABOVE Offensive lineman Bob Whitfield paved lanes for running backs and protected quarterbacks for 12 seasons in Atlanta.

Terance Mathis scored 57 touchdowns and tallied 7,349 yards in his eight years as a receiver in Atlanta.

GREATEST MOMENTS

26

PLAYOFF BOUND
12/24/1995

Falcons fans received an early Christmas gift when Atlanta stunned the 49ers in the Georgia Dome in the last week of the 1995 regular season. The Falcons, trailing 21-10 in the first half, were powered by two Morten Andersen field goals (28 and 59 yards) and two Terance Mathis touchdown catches slung by backup quarterback Bobby Hebert to complete the 28-27 comeback. (Hebert entered after starter Jeff George sprained his neck late in the first half.) Mathis grabbed a 37-yard pass to give the Falcons the go-ahead score, which allowed Atlanta to squeeze into the playoffs with a 9-7 record.

GREATEST MOMENTS

DIRTY BIRDS
11/8/1998

During a win at New England, the infamous Dirty Bird dance was created. Running back Jamal Anderson ran for 104 yards and two touchdowns to power the Falcons to a 41-10 drubbing of the Patriots. The Dirty Bird swept the NFL, as everyone from players to fans and even coaches began to show off their dance moves. It was just the beginning of Atlanta's greatest season in franchise history, which resulted in a Super Bowl appearance. Anderson carried the Falcons with an NFL-leading 410 rushes to go along with his 1,846 yards.

Jamal Anderson powers past New England linebacker Ted Johnson during Falcons 41-10 route of the Patriots in November 1998.

ABOVE Quarterback Bobby Hebert spent four seasons in Atlanta and earned his only Pro Bowl selection in 1993 after throwing a career high 24 touchdowns.

OPPOSITE Eric Metcalf was a wide receiver and kick returner for two seasons in Atlanta in the mid-1990s.

OPPOSITE Receiver Michael Haynes was a feared deep threat; he led the NFL in 1991 with 22.4 yards per catch.

ABOVE Shane Dronett records one of his two sacks on Panthers quarterback Kerry Collins in Week 5 of 1998. The second resulted in a fumble that was recovered by Lester Archambeau and led to a Morten Andersen field goal.

RING OF HONOR

GERALD RIGGS

PLAYED
1982–1988

INDUCTED
2013

Atlanta's current all-time leading rusher was the ninth overall pick in the 1982 NFL Draft, out of Arizona State. From the time he was drafted through the 1988 season, Gerald Riggs became known as a workhorse in the Falcons backfield, eclipsing 300 carries during three straight seasons, highlighted by an NFL-high 397 rushing attempts in 1985 en route to Riggs' first of three consecutive Pro Bowl appearances and a 1,719-yard year.

When all was said and done, Riggs became the all-time leading rusher for the Falcons in 1987 and finished his career in Atlanta a year later with 6,631 yards, a mark that has stood for 28 years.

When Riggs was traded in 1989 to Washington, it was a blessing for him, as in his final season in the league, in 1991, he scored six touchdowns in the postseason and help lead the Redskins to a 37-24 win over the Buffalo Bills in Super Bowl XXVI. In 2013, Riggs was inducted into the Falcons Ring of Honor.

Riggs could have never imagined his success with the Falcons, considering he had no idea they were going to draft him. "It was a big surprise, because I never spoke with anyone from the Falcons," he said.

Being inducted into the Falcons Ring of Honor three years ago was a special moment for Riggs. "I cherish being part of that group," he said. "I am identified with some of the finest football players in football, and I don't care what they say about Atlanta—there has been some really great players."

Chris Miller completes a pass to Erric Pegram in a 1991 game in San Francisco; the Falcons beat the rival 49ers twice that season.

GREATEST MOMENTS

BIRDS THWART NINERS
11/15/1998

After thumping the Patriots the week before, Atlanta returned home to host the star-studded San Francisco 49ers in Week 11. The Falcons jumped out to a 24-6 lead but found themselves leading by just five points late in the fourth quarter as Niners quarterback Steve Young hit Terrell Owens and Jerry Rice on long touchdown passes to tighten the game. Chris Chandler responded with a 78-yard bomb of his own to Terance Mathis with 2:51 remaining to seal the game for good at 31-19. Linebacker Jessie Tuggle returned a fumble for a score, and Jamal Anderson ran for 100 yards and two touchdowns in the victory.

GREATEST MOMENTS

29

REEVES RETURNS
1/9/1999

Head Coach Dan Reeves returned to the sidelines after a five-week absence and quadruple bypass heart surgery to coach the Falcons to a 20-18 Divisional Round win over the San Francisco 49ers, their second win in three matchups that season. The victory signified the first NFC Championship Game appearance in Atlanta history. Jamal Anderson once again powered his way through the 49ers defense en route to 113 yards and two scores. The Falcons defense harassed Steve Young into three interceptions, highlighted by a Eugene Robinson return of 77 yards to set up a Morten Andersen field goal.

Dan Reeves was hired as the Falcons head coach in 1997. The following year he led the team to the Super Bowl.

ABOVE Running back Craig Heyward gained 117 yards as the Falcons thumped the Rams 31-6 in November 1995.

OPPOSITE Jamal Anderson sat with teammate O.J. Santiago during a game against Carolina while the All-Pro running back was sidelined with a knee injury.

GREATEST MOMENTS

30

THE KICK
1/17/1999

In a play known simply as "The Kick," Morten Andersen nailed a game-winning 38-yard field goal in overtime against the Minnesota Vikings, lifting the Falcons to their first Super Bowl appearance with a 30-27 win. Atlanta rallied from down 10 in the fourth to force overtime on a 16-yard Terance Mathis catch with 57 seconds left. Chris Chandler stepped up when the Vikes slowed down Jamal Anderson, putting together his best performance all season, throwing for 340 yards and three touchdowns with no interceptions. With the win, Atlanta became the first dome team to ever make the Super Bowl.

Kicker Morten Andersen and holder Dan Stryzinski celebrate after Anderson scored the winning field goal in the Falcons overtime win over the Vikings, which sent Atlanta to the Super Bowl.

Head Coach Dan Reeves and Terence Mathis embrace after the Falcons' win in the NFC Championship.

GREATEST MOMENTS

31

BIRDS GO BOWLING
1/31/1999

The Falcons appeared in their first Super Bowl after a 14-2 regular season and narrow wins over San Francisco and Minnesota in the divisional and conference championship rounds. Morten Andersen got Atlanta on the scoreboard early in the first quarter against the Denver Broncos, but the Falcons found themselves trailing 17-6 at the half. Tim Dwight returned a kick 94 yards for a score in the fourth quarter, and Terance Mathis scored on a 3-yard reception, but Atlanta fell 34-19. Jamal Anderson rushed for 96 yards, while Mathis hauled in 85 yards receiving to lead the Dirty Birds.

CHAPTER 5

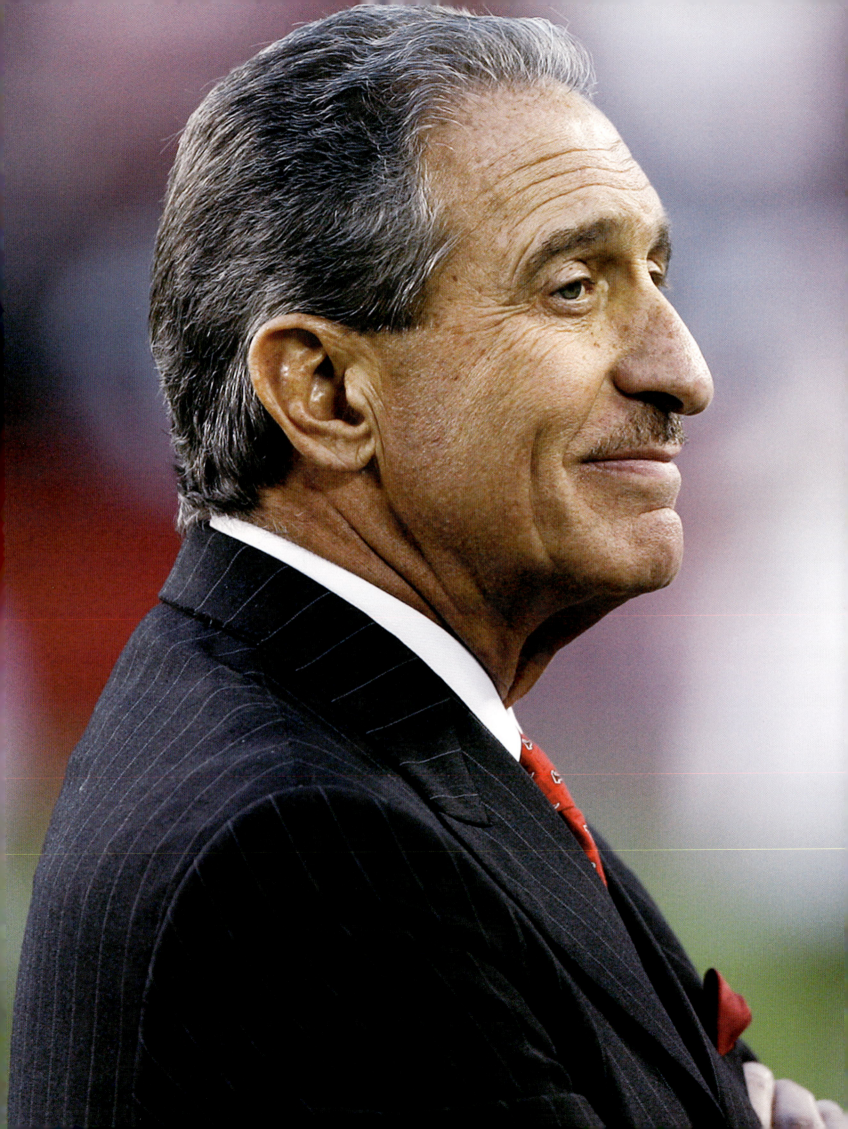

2000–2007

The dates on a calendar, the final seconds of a game, and a critical fourth down and goal do not shape a franchise. Only the actions performed within each moment can hold that authority. Challenges yield change, and then change yields new challenges. This process of empirical self-evolvement has driven the growth of the Falcons franchise over the past 50 seasons. Within the natural growing process, however, was the disparate era of 1999–2007, which concluded with a myriad of turmoil and adversity. Through equanimity, accountability, and the future-minded approach of new leadership, the franchise persevered. A period that staged some of the greatest obstacles for the franchise to overcome ultimately restructured the organization and set up the most successful run in team history.

The city of Atlanta exploded in the 1990s, and with the new millennium approaching, anything seemed possible. The Dirty Birds' 1998 run to Super Bowl XXXIII greeted the franchise with a previously unfamiliar limelight. In the aftermath of the 34-19 Super Bowl loss to Denver, however, the Lombardi Trophy was not the only remaining piece the franchise was missing.

As with each of the previous five years that followed winning seasons, the 1999 campaign was an opportunity for Atlanta to achieve back-to-back winning records for the first time. All-Pros and future Hall of Famers had led the Falcons throughout each of the previous four decades, the Falcons had achieved some of the NFL's most miraculous finishes throughout their history, and the taste of great individual seasons was always fresh enough to enchant a growing fan base along the way.

Sustaining success and the pursuit of consecutive winning seasons, however, continued to elude the franchise for another eight years before a bombardment of unexpected instability culminated in 2007. Adversity is not fixed; it is faced, and Atlanta's resolve in the face of adversity at the end of this post–Super Bowl XXXIII era allowed the franchise to achieve its long-desired culture of winning.

The bar was set high in 1999 as Atlanta looked to become the first team in NFL history to both host and play in the Super Bowl. A 1-6 start, however, derailed those aspirations, and the Falcons missed the playoffs with a 5-11 finish. But defensive end Patrick Kearney and center Todd McClure, drafted by the Falcons that year, began their development into franchise cornerstones that helped the team get back on track.

OPPOSITE Arthur M. Blank, co-founder of the Home Depot, purchased the Atlanta Falcons in 2002.

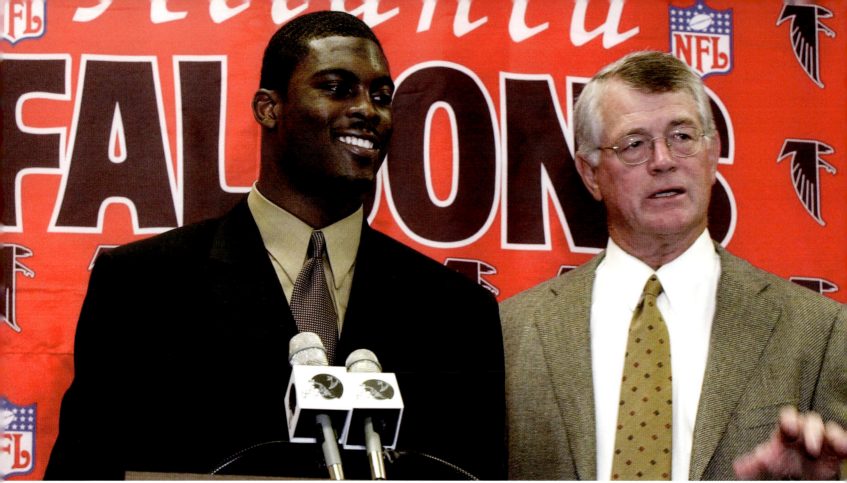

Nonetheless, the Super Bowl hangover spanned another year as the 2000 season resulted in a 4-12 finish. However, two career milestones, rather than the 252 points scored and 413 points allowed, characterized the season: It was Jessie Tuggle's 14th and final season, and his well-deserved farewell tour celebrated the inspiring and unforgettable career of "the Hammer." Also, wide receiver Terrance Mathis set a new team single-season record for receptions with 111, a mark later passed by Roddy White (115) in 2010 and shattered by Julio Jones (136) in 2015.

The Falcons, in need of offensive playmakers, aggressively pursued this emphasis heading into the 2001 draft. A trade with San Diego gave the Falcons rights to the No. 1 overall pick. Michael Vick became the first African American quarterback taken first in the NFL Draft, and the immediacy of the pick's excitement put Atlanta back in the spotlight. In the second round of the draft, former North Carolina tight end Alge Crumpler was taken off the board, beginning a career synonymous with success in Falcons annals. After a 6-4 start, however, the 2001 Falcons lost five of their final six games.

Vick earned just two starts in 2001, and the team's lone win in the final six weeks came in a 33-30 Week 15 home victory over the Buffalo Bills in front of a crowd of roughly 43,430 fans.

The week prior to the win over the Bills, however, marked one of the most significant moments in Atlanta Falcons history, gaining the team some momentum heading into the New Year. On December 17, 2001, it was announced that team president Taylor Smith would sell the team to Home Depot cofounder Arthur M. Blank for $545 million. It was a bittersweet day for Smith, who was handing over the franchise his father brought to the city 35 years before, but the franchise's founding family both trusted and admired Blank's vision, charisma, and philanthropic character.

"Our family has grown up in Falcons football, and it will be hard for us to let it go," said Smith. "We are proud to have found a rare opportunity to sell the team to Arthur, a high-caliber individual who has the passion and energy to enhance the franchise and solidify ownership of the Falcons in Atlanta for years to come."

ABOVE Head coach Dan Reeves shares the spotlight with the Falcons' top draft pick in 2001, Michael Vick, after Vick agreed to a six-year contract with Atlanta.

Blank gave the franchise a new leader and direction, but the team still needed its on-field commander. Vick was named the full-time starter for the 2002 season, and the saga began.

In hindsight, the rise and fall of the Vick era in Atlanta brings out an axiomatic assortment of emotions. However, the never-before-seen excitement and passion his play brought to the city of Atlanta and on a league-wide scale may never be replicated. Running back Warrick Dunn was signed in the 2002 offseason, and Vick centerpieced a fast and powerful running attack that paced the league and provided big-play potential on any given snap. Excitement grew as the Falcons took a 9-6-1 record into the playoffs, but the Falcons Fever was just getting started. In the wild card round, Vick and the Falcons stunned the football world, and the Brett Favre–led Packers, as they handed Green Bay its first-ever playoff loss in a 27-7 contest at Lambeau Field. The Falcons lost 20-6 in the divisional round to end the season, but Vick was named to the Pro Bowl and excitement surrounding the Falcons continued to skyrocket.

For the 2003 season, a brand-new look was unveiled as Blank's vision for the franchise was symbolized by a new Falcons logo with red and silver accents to depict a more powerful, aggressive falcon. New jersey designs were also introduced, and the Dome quickly filled with them. Vick broke a leg in the preseason, however, sapping the 2003 season, and Wade Phillips eventually replaced Head Coach Dan Reeves for the final eight games, which were split for a 5-11 finish.

The 2004 season was a fresh slate for Vick and the Falcons as first-time head coach Jim Mora Jr. took over. Atlanta opened the year with a 4-0 start and led the league with 2,672 rushing yards as an 11-5 regular season put the team back in the playoffs for the second time in three seasons. Atlanta steamrolled the visiting St. Louis Rams in the divisional round 47-17, as the offense compiled 327 rushing yards, a new single-game record for the franchise. Allen Rossum's 152 return yards set a new NFL postseason record, Vick set another league postseason record with his 119 rushing yards, and Dunn's 142 yards on the ground became the most in Falcons postseason history. Vick had led Atlanta back to the NFC Championship, but a 27-10 loss to Donovan McNabb and the Eagles ended the playoff run.

In 2005, the Falcons started 6–2, but injuries on the defensive side of the ball led to a 2-6 record in the second half of the season and the team lost its final three games to complete the 8-8 finish. The bright spots of the season included the Falcons going 3-0 in Monday Night Football appearances and stamping a 27-7 win over the Detroit Lions in what marked the franchise's first Thanksgiving Day game. The 2005 season also introduced a pair of franchise pillars, Jonathan Babineaux and Roddy White, through the draft.

The Falcons offense produced another explosive season in 2006, but a 2-7 finish the final nine weeks kept the Falcons out of the postseason with a 7-9 record, and Mora was fired following the season. But Vick became the first quarterback in modern NFL history to rush for over 1,000 yards in a season, with a record of 1,039 yards, in what turned out to be his final season in Atlanta. Dunn also eclipsed 1,000 yards with his team-high 1,140 rushing yards, and the duo became just the fourth pair of 1,000 rushers to lead a team since the AFL-NFL merger.

Atlanta turned to the University of Louisville's offensive-minded head coach, Bobby Petrino, who was hired as the franchise's 13th head coach on January 7, 2007. Petrino was brought in to maximize Vick's ability, but the illegal interstate dogfighting ring Vick was involved with and operated for five years sacked that partnership.

Vick was sentenced to 23 months in prison without ever taking a snap for Petrino, and on the Monday night of the sentencing, the Falcons suffered a 34-14 home loss to New Orleans that dropped the team record to 3-10. Petrino snuck back to the college ranks hours later, accepting the head coaching job at Arkansas, while only a four-sentence letter he left to the team announced his departure.

The way he left town with not so much as a face-to-face meeting with his players was hard for a team battling through tremendous adversity already. "The best way to describe the way we feel is betrayed and let down," Blank said in the subsequent press conference.

The emotions were strong, but so was the resolve the team and organization showed in the midst of the turmoil. The Falcons ended the season with a 44-41 win over the Seattle Seahawks, and the focus shifted to a fresh start in 2008 as the fans, the city, and the franchise embraced another new era.

NFL Commissioner Paul Tagliabue presents Michael Vick, the No. 1 overall pick in the 2001 NFL Draft, with a jersey from his new team.

GREATEST MOMENTS

32

THE VICK PICK
4/21/2001

Virginia Tech quarterback Michael Vick was the prize of the 2001 NFL Draft, but he would be long gone before the Falcons picked at No. 5. San Diego held the top pick, but when the Chargers could not agree to terms with Vick before the draft, they agreed to a trade with Atlanta for receiver Tim Dwight and the No. 5 selection (with which, the Chargers chose eventual league MVP LaDainian Tomlinson). Vick played six seasons in Atlanta, during which he led the Falcons to two playoff appearances, made three Pro Bowls, threw for 11,505 yards and 71 touchdowns, and ran for 3,859 yards and 21 scores.

GREATEST MOMENTS

BLANK BUYS BIRDS
12/6/2001

Over dinner at the Bones steakhouse in Buckhead, Arthur Blank, co-founder of Home Depot, reached an agreement with Taylor Smith, team president and the son of founder Rankin Smith, to purchase the team for $545 million. The purchase was approved unanimously by NFL owners. Under Blank's leadership, the Falcons have made the playoffs six times in 15 seasons and energized the fan base, selling out 110 of 112 regular season games, with eight consecutive sellout seasons through 2015.

Owner Arthur Blank welcomes new team president and general manager Rich McKay in December 2003. McKay was promoted to his current title of President and CEO in September 2011.

ABOVE Patrick Kerney wraps up Marc Bulger in Atlanta's 47-17 thrashing of the St. Louis Rams in the Divisional Round of the 2004 playoffs.

OPPOSITE Warrick Dunn springs free from a tackle in the Falcons 24-21 win over the Saints in November 2004.

RING OF HONOR

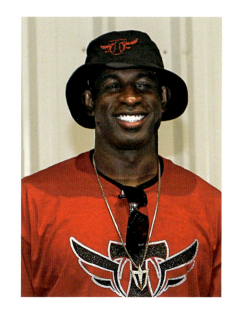

DEION SANDERS

PLAYED
1989–1993

INDUCTED
2010

Whatever you want to call Deion Sanders—"Prime Time" or "Neon Deion"—one word easily sums up the two-sport star's athletic career: electrifying. Sanders could do it all. The two-time consensus All-American was drafted fifth overall by the Atlanta Falcons in the 1989 NFL Draft after the New York Yankees plucked him in the 30th round of the 1988 MLB Draft.

Sanders, who played with the Falcons from 1989 to 1993, returned his first punt 68 yards for a touchdown in the 1989 season opener against the Los Angeles Rams, the first of Neon Deion's six punt-return touchdowns in his career. Defensively, he wrapped up his tenure with the Falcons with 24 of his 53 career interceptions.

Sanders' swagger and style on the field changed the game and paved the way for the lockdown corners and game-changing return men we see today.

"They don't pay nobody to be humble," boasted Sanders. "Some people will come out to see me do well. Some people will come out to see me get run over. But love me or hate me, they're going to come out."

Sanders' confidence was matched on and off the field, and he was never afraid to show it. "Water covers two-thirds of the Earth," said Sanders. "I cover the rest."

The 2011 Pro Football Hall of Fame inductee, who entered the Falcons Ring of Honor in 2010, is now a football analyst for the NFL Network.

OPPOSITE After 19 years in the NFL as an assistant coach, Jim Mora Jr. got his first head coaching job with the Falcons in 2004—and promptly led Atlanta to an 11-win season and the playoffs.

ABOVE T.J. Duckett celebrates a 4-yard touchdown run in a 27-10 win at Carolina by hammering a nail in the coffin.

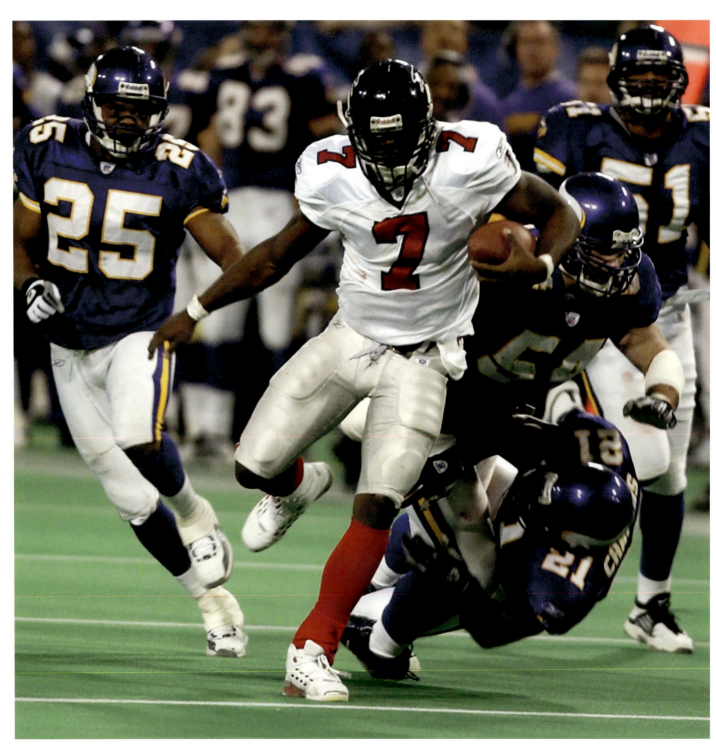
Michael Vick dusts four Vikings defenders on a 46-yard game-winning touchdown run in overtime December 2002.

GREATEST MOMENTS

34

SPEED KILLS
12/1/2002

In his first season as the starting quarterback, Michael Vick used his wheels consistently to give opposing teams headaches. He stunned the Vikings in Week 13 with a 46-yard overtime touchdown scamper to make the score 30-24, giving Atlanta eight straight games without a loss. The streak down the field remains one of the most iconic moments in NFL history, with the fleet-footed Vick splitting two defenders, causing them to collide. Vick accounted for 173 yards passing and one touchdown to go along with his 173 yards rushing and his two scores in Minnesota. The defense sacked Daunte Culpepper six times and intercepted three passes.

Michael Vick eludes a pack of Green Bay defenders in yet another highlight reel run, this in a Wild Card playoff game victory in January 2003.

GREATEST MOMENTS

35

HISTORY AT LAMBEAU
1/4/2003

The Falcons made NFL history by handing the Green Bay Packers their first playoff loss at legendary Lambeau Field in a 27-7 rout. Twenty-two-year-old Michael Vick came out victorious in the first playoff game of his young NFL career. As usual, Vick did it with both his arm and his legs, throwing for 117 yards and a touchdown while adding 64 rushing yards. Keion Carpenter came away with two interceptions off future Hall of Famer Brett Favre. Vick's performance put him on the national stage as one of the league's most dangerous players.

Michael Vick and Hall of Famer Brett Favre share a moment following the Falcons' 27-2 drubbing of the Packers in the playoffs in January 2003.

Falcons defensive back Keion Carpenter sports the Falcons new uniforms that debuted in 2003.

GREATEST MOMENTS

36

NEW-LOOK FALCONS
3/19/2003

The Falcons' new logo and new uniforms were unveiled during the offseason. The logo featured a sleeker, more aggressive bird that is displayed on the uniforms the Falcons wear to this day. With red highlights on the bird, the logo was fresh and dynamic while acknowledging the franchise's tradition and history. The logo was designed in conjunction with **NFL Properties** after a lengthy research process, which included conducting focus groups and polls with many fans. Atlanta has since turned more to red jerseys at home than black.

OPPOSITE Jonathan Babineaux and Chauncey Davis crunch Broncos quarterback Jay Cutler during a game in November 2008.

ABOVE Owner Arthur Blank looks on during a Falcons practice in Flowery Branch in July 2006.

ABOVE Cornerback DeAngelo Hall celebrates after a 37-yard pick-six interception return for a touchdown against the Arizona Cardinals in October 2006.

OPPOSITE Jessie Tuggle announces his retirement after 14 years as a Falcon. The five-time Pro Bowler still holds the franchise record for most tackles with 1,640.

GREATEST MOMENTS

37

DIVISION SUPREMECY
12/18/2004

Michael Vick made a clutch fourth-down conversion with a scramble as the Falcons defeat the Carolina Panthers 34-31 in overtime in Week 15 to clinch the third division title in team history. Vick threw for two scores and added one with his legs in the thrilling victory. Veteran running back Warrick Dunn gave the Panthers fits all day, rushing for 134 yards on 28 carries while punching in a score. The Falcons totaled four sacks, including one apiece from Keith Brooking and Patrick Kerney. Atlanta finished the season 11-5 to set up a Divisional Round matchup with the St. Louis Rams.

Carolina Panthers quarterback Jake Delhomme (top) was sacked four times and intercepted once in a Falcons 34-31 home victory in December 2004, while Atlanta's Warrick Dunn (bottom) rushed for 134 yards and a third quarter touchdown.

RING OF HONOR

JESSIE TUGGLE

PLAYED
1987–2000

INDUCTED
2004

The Falcons welcomed Jessie Tuggle, undrafted in 1987, to the franchise and opened the door to what would become one of the most productive careers the league has seen. From his rookie campaign to his farewell tour in 2000, he was a tackling machine at middle linebacker who led the NFL from 1990 to 1999 with 1,293 total tackles. Tuggle, who earned his nickname "the Hammer" with his bone-crushing hits, was named to the Pro Bowl five times and selected to the All-Pro team three seasons.

The Falcons made their first Super Bowl appearance in franchise history during the 1998 season after finishing with a winning record just twice in the 1990s. "That year really changed this franchise around," explained Tuggle.

Tuggle's leadership steered the magical run as Atlanta won its last nine games of the 1998 regular season after a 5-2 start. During a Week 10 win at New England, which ended a string of 22 straight losses at cold-weather stadiums, the infamous Dirty Bird dance was created as the Falcons handed the Patriots a 41-10 drubbing. Atlanta entered the playoffs as the No. 2 seed, where the team beat the rival 49ers, led by Steve Young and Jerry Rice, in the divisional round. The team shocked the football world the following week with an overtime victory over the 15-1 Vikings in the NFC Championship Game.

In 2004, Tuggle was inducted into the Falcons Ring of Honor with its inaugural class. Grady Jarrett, Tuggle's youngest son, was drafted by the Falcons in 2015, and his older son, Justin Tuggle, is a linebacker for the Houston Texans.

Return specialist Allen Rossum, who played for the Falcons from 2002 to 2006, holds the NFL record for career yards per touch with 18.2.

GREATEST MOMENTS

38

DOME DOMINATION
1/15/2005

After leading the NFL in rushing with 2,672 yards, Atlanta won its first NFC South title and took a bye into the playoffs, where the team hosted St. Louis in the Divisional Round. Atlanta dominated every facet of the game and shattered records in a 47-17 victory. The Falcons rushed for 327 yards (a new franchise record), Michael Vick rushed for 119 yards (a new NFL postseason mark for quarterbacks at the time), and Allen Rossum set a new NFL postseason record with 152 return yards. Warrick Dunn joined the history-making effort with 142 yards rushing, the most in Falcons postseason history.

GREATEST MOMENTS

39

NFL's LEADING SCORER
12/16/2006

Kicker Morten Andersen broke the NFL record to become the all-time leading scorer in NFL kicking history with an extra point, breaking Gary Anderson's record with 2,435 points. "The Great Dane" set the record on a nationally televised Saturday-night game during Week 15. Michael Vick scored four touchdowns in the game, but quarterback Tony Romo and running back Marion Barber were too much for the Falcons to contain, combining for four touchdowns themselves, and the Falcons fell to the Cowboys 38-28.

Morten Andersen is the Falcons all-time scoring leader with 806 points.

ABOVE Tight end Alge Crumpler scores the game-winning touchdown with :20 seconds left against Carolina in November 2007.

OPPOSITE Crumpler scored 35 touchdowns during the seven years he played in Atlanta.

CHAPTER 6

2008–Present

Before the 2008 season kicked off, an assemblage of new faces was brought in to oversee a plan to revitalize the franchise. Before the new blood was infused into the Falcon mainstream, however, another unambiguous change welcomed fans that year. A $300 million renovation to the Georgia Dome was completed as the color scheme inside and outside the building changed with a face-lift and a new paint job.

Gone was the original teal-and-maroon color scheme, replaced with a vibrant and lively red, black, and silver theme to match the team colors and subconsciously signify that new times lay ahead. The stadium's original teal seats were replaced with red ones in the 100 and 300 levels and black seats in the Verizon Wireless Club Level, while the entrance gates and concourses were also renovated and updated.

After a tumultuous 4-12 season in 2007, during which Head Coach Bobby Petrino left with three games remaining in his first season and journeyman quarterback Joey Harrington struggled to make the Falcons competitive, a change was made in the front office. Current Falcons CEO and team president Rich McKay decided to step down as general manager after four seasons, compiling a 30-34 record. For owner Arthur Blank, the search was now on to find the right man to succeed him. His pick, 41-year-old Thomas Dimitroff, had spent five years as director of college scouting for the New England Patriots from 2003 to 2007 and had been a part of their back-to-back Super Bowls in 2003 and 2004.

With Dimitroff's successful track record at a young age, Blank and company decided that he was the man for the job. Just 11 days in, the new general manager made the first splash during the year he won the Sporting News Executive of the Year award by hiring Mike Smith, defensive coordinator of the Jacksonville Jaguars.

"Mike possesses all of the key qualities we were looking for in a head coach," said Dimitroff to the press after landing his first head coach. "He has strong experience with winning teams, a track record of success, a solid, smart approach to the game, and high character and integrity."

The decision to hire Smith paid off immediately, as he won 11 games in his first year at the helm, but Smith couldn't have done it without a star quarterback. The Falcons swiped Boston College's Matt Ryan as the third overall pick in the 2008 draft. Ryan, a three-star quarterback coming out of Penn Charter School in Pennsylvania, skyrocketed up the draft boards after redshirting his freshman season. He steadily improved each year, passing for 1,514 yards as a sophomore, 2,942 as a junior, and 4,507 yards and 31 touchdowns as a senior while garnering recognitions such as First Team All-American, ACC Player of the Year, the Manning Award, and the Johnny Unitas Golden Arm Award.

OPPOSITE Dan Quinn became the 16th head coach of the Falcons in 2015.

A history of constant improvement was enough for the first-year GM to select the 6-foot-4 play caller. Desperate to make sure Ryan would stay upright, the Falcons traded two second-round picks and a fourth-rounder to move up to No. 21 overall in the first round, where they selected offensive tackle Sam Baker out of the University of Southern California. Much like Ryan, Baker was a proven commodity at the college level, collecting three straight First Team All-American selections in 2005–07 and helping his Trojans to a 34-5 record.

The final piece for the Falcons revamped offense was running back Michael Turner. On March 2, 2008, the Burner signed a six-year deal. The Falcons' ensuing success over the next five seasons has been unparalleled, as the team went 56-24 during 2008–2012.

The stretch of brilliance was sparked by Ryan's first pass—a 62-yard touchdown throw to Michael Jenkins. Atlanta went on to win 11 games with a rookie quarterback and a first-year head coach and general manager. Turner rushed for a Falcons single-season-record 17 touchdowns and galloped to 1,699 yards, third best in franchise history.

Following a 30-24 defeat in the wild card round to Arizona, Atlanta was faced with a familiar crossroads: Continue along a road toward the top of the league as a premier franchise, or push to build more momentum and create instant change. On April 23, 2009, Dimitroff landed a game changer that established the franchise as one that was serious about winning, trading a second-round pick for future Hall of Fame tight end Tony Gonzalez. Though the Falcons did not reach the 2009 playoffs, the team finished 9-7 and in the process marked its first back-to-back winning seasons.

Once again, Dimitroff won the Executive of the Year award from Sporting News. This time, the Falcons won the NFC South, their first division title since 2004. Atlanta finished 13-3 behind Roddy White's NFL-leading 115 receptions and NFC-best 1,389 yards, but in the divisional round, the Green Bay Packers, the eventual Super Bowl XLV champs, breezed past the Falcons 48-21.

For the first time, following a 10-6 regular season in 2011, Atlanta made the playoffs for a second consecutive season. Once again in the offseason, Dimitroff pulled the trigger on a franchise-changing move. The Falcons shipped

ABOVE Tony Gonzalez and Matt Ryan before a game in 2010, a year in which both made the Pro Bowl.

five draft picks to the Cleveland Browns on draft night to move up to No. 6 and select Julio Jones.

In a metaphorical roll of the dice, Atlanta gambled on the supremely talented wide receiver out of Alabama, and the team came out like bandits. Jones, who had 959 receiving yards as a rookie, has since blossomed into one of the league's best receivers, leading the NFL in catches (136) and yards (1,871) in 2015.

Putting a loss to the New York Giants in the wild card round behind them, the 2012 edition of the Falcons looked like a team on a mission. Atlanta opened with a franchise-best 8-0 record and clicked on all cylinders, as Ryan tossed 4,719 yards and 32 touchdowns, while both White and Jones both surpassed 1,100 yards and Gonzalez collected 930 yards.

The Falcons rolled to 13-3 overall, a third-straight playoff appearance, and the team's second division title in three years. The Seattle Seahawks were welcomed to the Georgia Dome on January 13 for the divisional round, a game not soon to be forgotten. Atlanta jumped out to a 27-7 lead heading into the fourth quarter and looked unstoppable. Ryan hit Gonzalez, White, and Jason Snelling for touchdowns, but the Seahawks still had 15 minutes remaining to make a comeback. Russell Wilson orchestrated 21 unanswered points, capped by Marshawn Lynch's 2-yard touchdown plunge with 31 seconds left, to give Seattle a 28-27 lead.

The atmosphere was uncomfortably tense after evaporation of a commanding lead, but, as they had so many times before, Matty Ice and Matt Bryant kept their cool. Ryan marched the Falcons down to the Seattle 31-yard line with 13 seconds left, setting up a Bryant field goal attempt. Bryant drove home the 49-yarder with eight seconds left to clinch a 30-28 win, his third game winner of the season.

In the conference championship, the Falcons had one more opportunity for some late-game heroics, but, trailing 28-24 behind the San Francisco 49ers, Atlanta couldn't find the end zone from 10 yards out with 1:13 left, and the 49ers preserved their lead.

The Falcons missed out on the postseason for each of the three seasons following the heartbreaking loss to San Francisco. The aging pieces of the 2012 roster were let go, leading to change among the core players outside of Ryan, White, and Jones. Atlanta, stumbling to 10-22 over the next two seasons, decided to part ways with Coach Smith after the 2014 season and a 66-46 record, the franchise's most wins for a single coach.

The 2015 season brought optimism and exuberance among the organization and fan base as Dan Quinn was selected to be the franchise's 16th head coach. Quinn came over after guiding the Seattle Seahawks to two Super Bowl appearances and winning Super Bowl XLVIII.

Quinn quickly got to work alongside Dimitroff as they determined that the No. 8 pick in the 2015 NFL Draft would be pass rusher Vic Beasley Jr. The team's new fast and physical mind-set paid early dividends as the team started 5-0. Second-year running back Devonta Freeman emerged as a Pro Bowler out of new offensive coordinator Kyle Shanahan's backfield, amassing 1,639 total yards and a league-high 11 rushing touchdowns.

After a 5-0 start, the Falcons leveled for an 8-8 finish in their 50th season, but in Week 16, they scored a 20-13 win over the 15-0 Carolina Panthers in front of a raucous home crowd.

Fifty years of Falcons football has brought amazing storylines, moments, and obstacles the organization, the city, and fans have faced. The next fifty years are sure to see even more change as an era unlike any other quickly approaches.

The state-of-the-art Mercedes-Benz Stadium, set to open in 2017, will be the crown jewel of the city and the sports world. The 310-by-385-foot, one-of-a-kind retractable-roof oval will open like the Oculus in the Pantheon of Rome while encased by a five-story, 360-degree high-definition video halo board, the first of its kind in the world. Out of the northeast corner, natural sunlight will beam through a floor-to-ceiling window to illuminate the field with the backdrop of the beautiful skyline of downtown Atlanta.

It began as a dream in the 1960s to bring a franchise to the city, resulting in a franchise born from a commitment to reach the unthinkable. This foundation has written the past while it drives the future of the Atlanta Falcons.

GREATEST MOMENTS

40

FACE OF THE FRANCHISE
4/26/2008

The Falcons used the No. 3 pick of the 2008 NFL Draft to select Boston College quarterback Matt Ryan. Ryan's impact was immediate and steady as he became the first Falcons rookie quarterback in franchise history to throw for over 3,000 yards in a season—and threw a touchdown on his first NFL pass. He finished 2008 with 3,440 passing yards, 17 touchdowns (one rushing), and 11 interceptions while earning AP Rookie of the Year honors. In 2013, prior to entering the final season of his rookie contract, the record-setting QB agreed to a five-year extension to stay a Falcon.

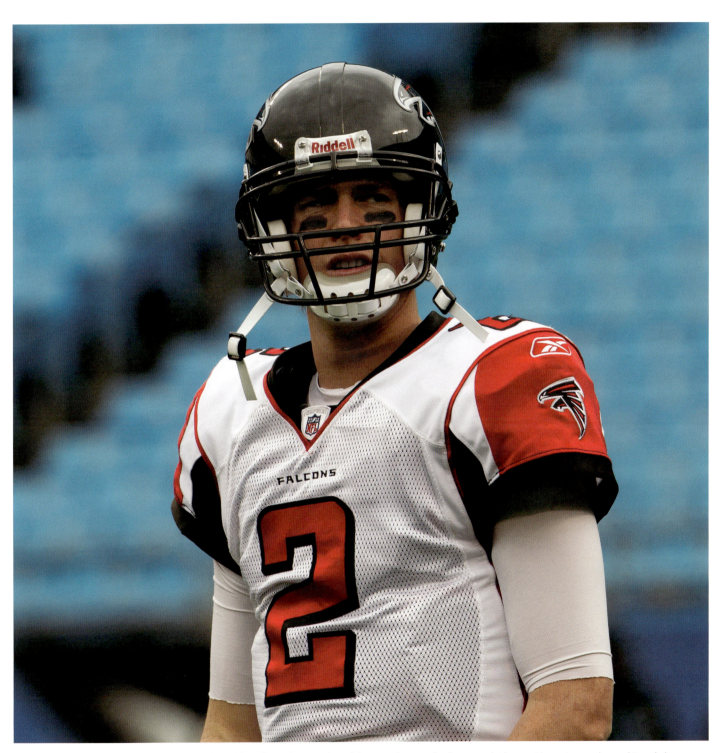
In eight seasons as a Falcon, quarterback Matt Ryan has set franchise passing marks for completions, attempts, yards, and touchdowns.

Running back Michael Turner scores (top) against the Detroit Lions in the 2008 season opener. Nicknamed "The Burner," Turner was all smiles (bottom) after setting a team record in that game with 220 rushing yards.

GREATEST MOMENTS

41

TURNER BREAKS RECORD
9/7/2008

Opening the season with the Detroit Lions in 2008, recently signed running back Michael Turner exploded for a franchise-record 220 yards—also an NFL record for the most rushing yards in a player's first game with a new team. Turner started his day off hot when he took a first-quarter handoff 66 yards to the house. He wasn't done. On the very next drive, he reached the end zone again on a five-yard carry. If it weren't for a penalty, he would have had three rushing touchdowns in the game. The huge day from Turner and the win propelled Atlanta to an 11-5 season and a wild card berth.

GREATEST MOMENTS

42

BACK-TO-BACK
1/3/2009

The 9-7 Falcons notched their first back-to-back winning seasons in franchise history, finishing the year with three straight wins, including a road victory in the final game over Tampa Bay 20-10 in Week 17. With the game tied at 10 early in the final quarter, Matt Ryan constructed a drive that culminated in hitting Roddy White for a 12-yard score with 7:18 remaining. Matt Bryant iced the game with a 36-yard field goal with a minute left. Jason Snelling was the workhorse back in place of an injured Michael Turner, running for a career-high 147 yards in the win. Ryan threw for 22 touchdowns during the year, while Turner ran for 871 yards in 11 games.

A 2005 first-round draft pick from Alabama-Birmingham, Roddy White leads all Falcons receivers in career games, receptions, yards, and touchdowns.

ABOVE Defensive end John Abraham enjoyed the best season of his 14-year career as a Falcon in 2008 when he recorded a career-high 16.5 sacks.

OPPOSITE Linebacker Curtis Lofton sacks San Francisco quarterback Alex Smith in a 16-14 Falcons win on October 2010.

GREATEST MOMENTS

DRAFT DAY MAGIC
4/28/2011

At the 2011 NFL Draft on Apr. 28, Atlanta traded five draft picks to move up to No. 6 overall and select Alabama wide receiver Julio Jones. The risky move ended up paying dividends, as Jones totaled 959 yards receiving his rookie season and tacked on eight touchdowns. General Manager Thomas Dimitroff pulled the trigger on the move that gave Matt Ryan two premier wide receivers outside. Teaming up Jones with Roddy White (and tight end Tony Gonzalez) gave the Falcons one of the most potent passing attacks in the league. Jones has since appeared in two Pro Bowls.

A Pro Bowler in three of his first five years in the league, Julio Jones (top and bottom) had a monster year in 2015, leading the NFL with 136 receptions and 1,871 yards. Jones holds the NFL record for career receiving yards per game with an average of 95.4.

Deion Sanders poses with his bust upon his induction into the Pro Football Hall of Fame in 2011.

GREATEST MOMENTS

44

PRIMED FOR THE HALL
8/6/2011

Deion Sanders made history as the first Pro Football Hall of Famer to enter the prestigious group as an Atlanta Falcon. Sanders was the fifth pick overall in the 1989 NFL Draft by Atlanta, where he played until 1993. During his time in Atlanta, he intercepted 24 passes, including a career-high seven in 1993, three of which he returned for touchdowns. His five years with the Falcons saw Sanders find the end zone 10 times (three defensive plays, three kick returns, two punt returns, and two receptions). Sanders was named an All-Pro eight times in his career.

GREATEST MOMENTS

45

EIGHT IS GREAT
11/4/2012

Behind four field goals from Matt Bryant and 342 yards passing from Matt Ryan, the Falcons improved their record to 8-0 and became the last undefeated team in the NFL. Despite being down 6-0 to Dallas going into the second quarter, Atlanta—on two Bryant field goals, including one with time expiring—tied the game up going into the half. A Michael Turner rushing touchdown broke the tie moments into the fourth quarter. The Cowboys scored a late touchdown, but yet another Bryant field goal with 17 seconds remaining sealed the 19-13 victory.

Kicker Matt Bryant booted field goals measuring 45, 46, 36, and 32 yards in a November 2012 home victory against the Cowboys.

Cornerback Desmond Trufant is all business during a late season game at Carolina in 2015.

Guard Justin Blalock clears the way for running back Jacquizz Rodgers against the Vikings in September 2014.

GREATEST MOMENTS

46

BRYANT SINKS SEATTLE
1/13/2013

Trailing Seattle by a point with under a minute to play in a 2012 divisional playoff game at the Georgia Dome, quarterback Matt Ryan drove Atlanta downfield with two long completions to set the table for a 49-yard Matt Bryant field goal attempt with just eight seconds left on the clock. The Falcons had just watched a 27-7 fourth-quarter advantage evaporate as the Seahawks scored 21 unanswered points to take the lead with just 31 seconds remaining. But Bryant's long kick was perfect, sending the packed house into a frenzy and cementing an **NFC Championship appearance at the Dome one week later.**

Matt Bryant celebrates with the game-winning ball after kicking a 49-yard field goal with less than a minute remaining to defeat Seattle in the 2012 playoffs.

Tony Gonzalez and Falcons owner Arthur Blank embrace during a halftime ceremony honoring the all-time great tight end prior to his retirement after the 2013 season.

GREATEST MOMENTS

47

ONE OF A KIND
12/29/2013

Tony Gonzalez is arguably the greatest tight end to ever play the game. He ranks second on the all-time receptions list, sixth in receiving touchdowns, and fifth in receiving yards, and these honors rank him first among tight ends. In his final game, he ran 56 yards on four receptions in a 21-20 loss to the Carolina Panthers. During halftime, the Falcons presented Gonzalez with a half-Chiefs, half-Falcons helmet to commemorate his 17-year career with both organizations. In his final season, Gonzalez still put up big numbers, with 859 yards receiving, 83 receptions, and eight touchdown catches.

GREATEST MOMENTS

48

CLAUDE'S DAY
8/2/2014

Defensive end **Claude Humphrey**, who holds the franchise record with six **Pro Bowl** appearances, was inducted into the **NFL H**all of Fame after a **10-**year career in **Atlanta** and three seasons in **Philadelphia**. In 1978, he was a part of the first team in **Falcon** history to make the playoffs. Humphrey, who started in 99 games while in **Atlanta,** was one of the most feared rushers in the league—and was also able to stuff the run. He totaled 126.5 sacks and caused two safeties. In 1968, he was named the **NFL Defensive** Rookie of the Year, and he continued to improve his play every year.

Claude Humphrey delivers a heartfelt speech during his induction into the Pro Football Hall of Fame in 2014.

OPPOSITE Linebacker Sean Weatherspoon, who played from 2010 to 2013 with Atlanta, rejoined the Falcons for the 2016 season.

ABOVE General Manager Thomas Dimitroff made moves in the draft and free agency that Falcons fans hope will result in a return to the playoffs in 2016.

Devin Hester finished his electrifying career as a Falcon in 2015.

GREATEST MOMENTS

49

HESTER'S SPRINT TO HISTORY
9/18/2014

Atlanta took a 56-0 lead in the third quarter before handing visiting Tampa Bay a 56-14 loss in Week 3, but a new NFL record set by All-Pro return man Devin Hester defined the game. Hester opened the second quarter with a 20-yard touchdown run and minutes later took a punt 62 yards for his record-breaking 20th career return touchdown (and his 14th career punt-return touchdown). Deion Sanders, who had held the record with 19 return touchdowns, was there calling the Thursday night game for the NFL Network and provided an inspirational moment when he congratulated Hester.

GREATEST MOMENTS

50

BREAKING GROUND
5/19/2014

On May 19, the Falcons officially broke ground on an iconic new retractable-roof stadium that is set to open in 2017 and will cost over $1.4 billion to construct. The stadium, which will also be home to the new Major League Soccer franchise Atlanta United FC, will host NCAA Final Fours, NCAA football, and eventually a Super Bowl. Atlanta will now house the largest LED scoreboard in the world, one three times bigger than the current record holder, which was installed at EverBank Field in Jacksonville.

Mercedes-Benz Stadium will become the new home to the Atlanta Falcons in 2017.

SKYBOX PRESS

Publisher
Peter Gotfredson

Design
Nate Beale/SeeSullivan

Editor
Scott Gummer

Copyeditor
Mark Nichol

Writers
I.J. Rosenberg
Craig Sager II
Kyle Sandy

SKYBOX PRESS wishes to thank Greg Beadles, Brett Jewkes, Morgan Shaw Parker, Brian Cearns, Matt Haley, Sammie Burleson, Beth Auer, Melissa Altman, and Jim Smith; Mary Kirchner, Lynette Washington, Marlon Copeland, and Nancy, Drew & the Miller Family; Joe Vanderzanden, Pat Sommers, and Kevin Toyama.

PHOTOGRAPHY:

ATLANTA FALCONS: Jimmy Cribb, Mike Benford, and Kevin Liles

ASSOCIATED PRESS: NFL Photos, Lois Bernstein, Spencer Weiner, Paul Abell, Dave Pickoff, Horace Cort, Joe Holloway, Harry Cabluck, Steve Helber, Charles Kelly, Arthur Anderson, Ric Feld, Carl Viti, Jim Mone, H. Joe Holloway, Jr., Eric Risberg, Judy Ondrey, Peter Moran, Jeff Reinking, Amy Sanscettes, Olga Shalygin, John Dickerson, Doug Mills, Werner Slocum, John Bazemore, Winslow Townson, Jonathan Daniel, Ed Reinke, Curtis Compton, Ross D. Franklin, Mark Lennihan, Tom Olmscheid, Darren Hauck, Erik S. Lesser, Chuck Burton, Dave Martin, and Shawn Wood

Copyright © 2016 by Atlanta Falcons Football Club, LLC

All rights reserved. No part of this book may be reproduced in any form without written permission from the publisher.

www.skyboxpress.com
info@skyboxpress.com
(877) 632-8558

ISBN: 978-0-9964553-1-2

Printed in the United States of America

10 9 8 7 6 5 4 3 2 1

Published by Skybox Press, an imprint of Luxury Custom Publishing, LLC.